Finding My Voice

DIANE REHM

Finding My Voice

CAPITAL
BOOKS, INC.

Capital Books, Inc.
P.O. Box 605
Herndon, Virginia 20172-0605

ISBN 1-892123-90-8 (alk. paper)
A hardcover edition of this book was originally published
in 1999 by Alfred A. Knopf. It is here reprinted by
arrangement with the author.
First Capital Books, Inc., trade paperback edition published 2002.

Library of Congress Cataloging-in-Publication Data
Rehm, Diane.
Finding my voice / by Diane Rehm.
p.   cm.
ISBN 1-892123-90-8 (alk. paper)
1. Rehm, Diane.
2. Radio broadcasters—United States—Biography.
I. Title.
PN1991.4.R438A3   2002
791.44'028'092—dc21
[B]   20011058339

Printed in the United States of America on acid-free paper
that meets the American National Standards
Institute z39-48 Standard.

First Edition
10   9   8   7   6   5   4   3   2

This book is dedicated to
John "Scoop" Rehm,
lover, teacher, and, finally, best friend.

Contents

Finding My Voice

INTRODUCTION

*A*S I BEGIN this effort, John is in Kampala and the house is still. It's Sunday, the neighborhood is quiet, and the only sounds are those of birds and the breeze blowing through the leaves of the divided maple tree just outside our bedroom window. Silence unnerves me. I am uncomfortable in it. It's as though I don't fully exist in silence. I walk into our home and my first action is to turn on the radio, hoping that the sound of a human voice will lift me out of my discomfort and fear. As I grow older, I become increasingly aware of how difficult a factor silence has been in my life, and the extent to which the sounds of radio have helped me to address that difficulty. Even as I work at my office desk in the afternoons, there is music playing in the background. The sounds fill the void in me, a void that reminds me again and again of just how close I am to being alone. Silence equals aloneness.

After more than twenty-five years in radio and many more

years with radio as a constant companion, it nevertheless surprises me how important a factor it is and always has been in my life. From my earliest days listening to soap operas and daily adventure series, I've been affected by the voices coming across the airwaves. First of all, the sound, or tone. Is it friendly, is it warm, is it inviting? How well does the voice I'm listening to communicate information? Is there a particular accent, a curious word pronunciation? What about the inflections, the words that are emphasized? The voice creates an image in my mind to which I'm drawn, or from which I turn away.

When I was a child, the sound of my mother's voice could fill me with joy or make me cringe. I knew by her tone whether I was welcome in her presence or not. I knew also when the silence that filled our home wasn't to be interrupted. By contrast, the voices coming across the radio held for me a magic that was not to be found in my own household, a kind of friendliness and warmth that I could count on. The characters in "The Lone Ranger," "The Green Hornet," or "Our Gal Sunday" were all people who wouldn't turn on me, nor would they leave me in silence, making me question my very right to exist.

That I should have been so fortunate as to have found a career in the medium to which I've been drawn all my life—where I could, presumably, keep the sound going—seems miraculous. But now, after all these years of effortlessly using my voice on the air, I have learned that I'm afflicted with a rare neurological disorder called spasmodic dysphonia. It's a condition that creates a strangled hoarseness, fills my voice with tremors, and makes me sound like a very old woman. It requires periodic injections of botulinum toxin into my vocal cords, which leave me without a voice, with only the faintest whisper, for weeks at a time.

It began in 1991. Though I was keenly aware of it at the time, I didn't begin to seek the help of speech therapists, neurologists, and otolaryngologists until 1994. Again and again, I was told that there was basically nothing wrong with my voice that appropriate breathing couldn't cure. I worked hard at voice therapy but eventually became frustrated because of the lack of progress. Throughout that period, I questioned why this was happening to me at this time in my life, after so many years of being on the air without any concerns for my voice. Was it the stress of success? Was it a psychological disorder I was inflicting on myself? Was I punishing myself for somehow failing to win my mother's love, for failing in a brief first marriage, and even, at times, for not living up to my expectations for myself as a wife and mother? After all the psychological therapy I'd been through in my life, why were these problems now coming back to haunt me? I may never fully know the answers to those questions. But in setting them down on paper, perhaps I can learn to hear the responses coming from within me. In my lifelong fear of silence, I may have missed learning to listen carefully to my own internal voice, so concerned have I been with those coming from outside myself.

My mind drifts back to those early days of punishment in my bedroom, when my mother's wrath is expressed in silence. I am eight or nine. I look out the window of my childhood bedroom, at the old shed in the woods across the alley. I pace the room, trying to count the floorboards, appraising each knot, measuring the distance between the wall and the edge of the carpet, tracing with my finger each flower basket on the wallpaper. I talk to myself, trying to understand how I could've gotten myself into such trouble—again. I'm never sure exactly what actions have led her to confine me to my room and turn away from me. I only know that when the moment descends, there is no turning back. I listen for sounds throughout the house. I know she's in the kitchen starting dinner, or in the basement washing clothes, or in the den listening to the radio. I yearn to be with her, but I know I'm not welcome in any of those places.

Everyone who sees her says how pretty she is. Slender, a little over five feet tall, she has fair skin, hazel eyes, and auburn hair. But the sound of my voice makes her face go sour. Her eyes narrow, the muscles in her cheekbones grow taut, her back stiffens. I am not welcome in her presence because I've done something to displease her. Sometimes I wonder whether it's my very existence that displeases her. She doesn't laugh with me very often. Am I the girl child she didn't want? It's a question I began asking myself many years ago. It will be days, and sometimes weeks, before she speaks to me again. The silence is so deep.

When we do, finally, return to a point where talk is permitted, there are few subjects open for discussion. Conversation between my parents takes place at dinner (she prepares the meal while he sits at the table in the kitchen; as he eats, she moves about the room, offering second helpings). I try to understand how our family operates, what is important, and what it is that makes my mother happy. She listens as my father tells her about his day, making occasional comments, laughing softly. I hear fragments referring to the stock market, a favorite customer at the grocery store he owns with two of my uncles, snippets referring to my aunts or uncles, to rising costs, and indirect references to outstanding bills. I sit very quietly, listening but not talking. The conversation is never intended to include me. It's as though I'm not there.

There is much about my life I don't know or can't understand. I wonder if there are others who have such dim recollections of their pasts. Perhaps if I force myself to concentrate on my family and expose my thoughts to the light of my own vision, then I can begin to make some sense of it all. And perhaps the exploration itself will provide me with answers to questions I've had but never dared to ask.

Part One

OTHER VOICES

CHAPTER 1

*T*O THIS DAY, I have no reliable account of how my parents came to be with and love each other. Their mutual affection was always apparent, and yet they never talked about their beginnings. The circumstances that brought Eugenie Zouekie and Wadie Aed together have always been clouded in a haze of mystery, with the truth, whatever it might have been, quite probably more straightforward and understandable than my imaginings or the stories I've heard. What I do know is that my father's family was apparently fairly well off, supported by my grandfather, Solomon Aed, who was a tailor by profession. He and his wife, Nazha, lived in the city of Mersin, Turkey, located on the shore of the Mediterranean Sea. They were Christians, part of the Eastern Orthodox community. There were three brothers—George, Toufic, and Wadie—and four sisters—Victoria, Julia, and twins Fahima and Wadia.

Theirs was a secure life, in a comfortable home. But according to an oral history given by Wadia to her grandson, Richard Haj-jar, their mother constantly talked of coming to America. "Even with the secure life that we had in Mersin," said Wadia, "my mother always had it in her heart to come to the free country of America. She was quite willing to sacrifice her life in Mersin to come to the freedom she had always dreamed about." Those of us who take life in this country for granted cannot fully appreciate the yearnings of those like my father's family, believing as they did that an opportunity to live here was worth so much effort and hardship.

My father's oldest brother, George, who was seventeen at the time, came to this country in 1907. The second-oldest brother, Toufic, came in 1909. My father, Wadie, and one of his sisters, Victoria, came two years later. The plan was for the oldest children to go first so they could become acquainted with America, learn the language, and begin to build a life. Their parents had given them a sufficient amount of money on which to get a good start.

The rest of the family now waited their turn to go to America, but they had to be sure that the brothers could provide for the entire group. My father and his brothers wrote frequently, relating stories of their success in obtaining work in the shoe factories of Auburn, New York, supporting themselves and putting money aside. Finally, in 1913, my father sent word to his family in Mersin that he had made the arrangements for them to come. His parents and the three remaining sisters got ready for the trip, with no certainty of just how long the voyage would be. After weeks of preparation, they left Mersin and made the three-day voyage to Beirut, Lebanon. There they were to undergo medical examinations by an American doctor to gain admission to the U.S., but they were forced to turn back because my grandfather had an eye infection. Later that year, they tried again, this time traveling from Mersin to Naples, Italy. Sadly, the infection had persisted and they were turned away a second time. They remained in Italy for a month, hoping the infection would clear, but unfortunately it didn't and they were forced to return to Mersin once again, expecting to attempt the trip again sometime the following year. But World War I intervened in August 1914. All visas to the U.S. were cut off. Meanwhile, my father and his brother Toufic, having become American citizens, were drafted into the U.S. Army.

It was not until 1921 that the family finally succeeded in making the voyage to this country. They sailed from Petros, Greece, to the U.S. For one month, they saw nothing but water and sky, impatiently anticipating sight of Ellis Island. "All of a sudden," said Wadia, "there was a great cheer from the many immigrants on board. I caught my first glimpse of America. My mother stood in silence with tears of joy streaming from her eyes. Then, as my mother slowly stepped off the ship, she kneeled and very solemnly kissed the ground." At Ellis Island, they were all taken to a dormitory where they stayed overnight, awaiting yet another medical examination. They were met there by my father, whom they hadn't seen for ten years, and he assured them that everything would be fine. After passing the medical exam, they went before a judge to swear that their tickets had been paid for and that they had dollars with them. My father had to show that he had five thousand dollars in the bank to take care of the family. After this was done, the judge granted the family the necessary papers and informed them that they were the last five people to be allowed to come to America from Turkey. They had filled the quota.

It has been more difficult to learn exactly how my father and his brothers spent the years in this country before the rest of the family arrived. What I do know is that the eldest, George, went directly to Auburn, followed by his brothers and sister. They went to work in one of Auburn's shoe factories, supporting themselves and putting money aside, with a dream of someday starting their own business. I can only assume that they went to

Auburn because they had friends there who could help them find jobs and begin to get on their feet.

After several years, George, along with his new bride, Annette, decided to move to Washington, D.C., leaving behind his life as a factory worker. How much money he had saved by this time I can't know, but it was sufficient to allow him to open a shoe repair shop of his own on Wisconsin Avenue in Georgetown. Later, he would purchase his first grocery store at Ninth and S Streets NW. Shortly thereafter, my father, Wadie, and my uncle Toufic came to Washington together with their sister Victoria and her new husband, Alexander. My father and Toufic purchased and operated a small grocery store on New Hampshire Avenue NW, and it was at this point, I believe, that my father decided to return to the old country in search of my mother.

There are several versions of their meeting. One account is that the two were born in the same town in Mersin, and that Eugenie was promised to Wadie at birth. He was thirteen years her senior, and their parents were good friends. The second account (according to my sister, Georgette) is that my father had met Eugenie's parents before he left Turkey to come to the United States, and that an agreement had been reached among them that he would return for her once he'd made his fortune. So Wadie set off on a journey back to Mersin to marry Eugenie. But when he got there, he learned that Eugenie had moved with her family to Alexandria, Egypt, and that she had become engaged to someone else. By all accounts, she was deeply in love with her fiancé, but under pressure from her family, she broke her engagement, married Wadie, and returned with him to the United States in 1929.

Their formal wedding portrait shows a slender couple with clear eyes looking directly into the camera, slight smiles on each of their faces. She wears a simple, long, sheer, sleeveless wedding dress, scooped at the bodice. A sheer caplike veil covers her head, with her dark bangs protruding. She carries a large and beautiful bouquet of orchids and lilies of the valley, long streamers of ribbon descending onto her gown. She was twenty-two. He was thirty-five. My father's dark eyes and heavy eyebrows initially draw attention away from the fact that he is nearly bald, having lost most of his hair in his twenties.

It's impossible to know whether it was a happy day for Eugenie. It was a day that meant she would be uprooted from all that she knew and loved, to follow my father across the ocean to Washington, D.C. The transition to life in the United States can't have been easy for her. As the youngest in her family, she had enjoyed the comfort and security of living with, or near to, her mother, her brother, and her sister, as well as nieces and nephews and everything that was dear to her. She married my father, perhaps against her will, and entered an already tight-knit family whose women eyed her suspiciously, even jealously. Winning the affections of my father's brothers was easy; his sisters were another matter. Perhaps there was a certain possessiveness on their part over my father, who was their youngest brother.

I wish I could have seen my mother in her youth. I wish I could have heard the sound of her voice. There's a photograph of her, stretched out across large boulders in what appears to be Rock Creek Park in Washington. She's smiling and happy, a young woman enjoying herself and content to be admired by the person holding the camera. Eugenie brought with her from Egypt an innate sense of style and fashion. She cared about the clothes she wore, many of which she made, as well as her hairstyle and makeup. Her appearance didn't reflect the Old World, and therefore seemed quite different from that of the other women in the family of which she had just become a part. She was endowed with a shapely but trim figure that must have been the envy of her newly acquired sisters-in-law. The story of my mother's brassiere is an indication of just how far those feelings of rivalry were carried. I learned about this incident only recently, and it supports the impression I had through my childhood years, that my mother had reason to be wary of my father's sisters.

One of my cousins, Louise Hajjar, was a child of four or five in 1930, the year after my mother came to this country. Her mother, Wadia, and Wadia's twin sister, Fahima, noticed that my mother was wearing a type of undergarment they had never seen before, a brassiere. Both were apparently very envious, but rather than ask Eugenie about it directly, they resorted to a dirty trick. According to Louise, the two sisters waited until my mother had left the apartment where she and my father were living at the time to do some errands. Then, while one of the twins kept watch, the other slipped in and "borrowed" the brassiere. It had been hand-stitched by Eugenie, copying a garment she had seen. Hurriedly, the two attempted to figure out how to reproduce it. They removed my mother's hand stitches, took the bra apart, and created a pattern from the fragments. With the glee of two successful conspirators, they managed to put it back together again and return it to its drawer before my mother got home.

I was amazed when I heard the story, not only at such blatant thievery but also at having objective confirmation of what my mother was up against. The twin sisters often talked and laughed together about the incident, regarding it as one of the more successful stunts they'd pulled off as a team. Having overheard their conversation, Louise was warned in very stern language that she must never, ever repeat the tale of the stolen bra. Telling me the story more than sixty years later, Louise said, felt like an act of betrayal, an act she would never have committed had the perpetrators been alive.

There's another example of how difficult life must have been for Eugenie, and it's a story that has haunted me. In fact, I'm not sure where or how I learned of this incident. In my recollection, my mother told me the story, but it seems out of character for her to have shared something so personal with me. Yet I've known the story for so long, and felt her anguish so deeply, I can only trust that, in some moment of vulnerability, she shared it with me. Apparently someone, perhaps one of the aunts, convinced my mother that her eyelashes were unattractive. As I write this, in an age when cosmetic companies spend millions of dollars to promote the look of long, thick, beautiful lashes, it's hard to believe that anyone would say such a thing, or, more importantly, could convince a woman that the lovely fringe surrounding the most interesting part of her face could possibly be undesirable. But that is what was done. Whether to please her tormentor or because she was naïve enough to believe what she was told, my mother allowed her eyelashes to be cut off. Did she weep? Did she complain to my father? Was she angry? Was she depressed? I cannot know.

CHAPTER 2

*M*Y SISTER, Georgette, was born on July 28, 1931, two years after Eugenie and Wadie married. By this time, my father and his brother Toufic and their brother-in-law, Alexander, had together purchased a grocery store at Nineteenth and Wyoming Avenue NW. I have no idea how Eugenie felt about her status in life, her motherhood, and almost no photographs to offer a clue, since cameras were not the ever-present accessory they have become today. I do recall a single photograph of her nursing my sister, smiling unselfconsciously as she offered a breast to her infant.

The baffling part of both my sister's and my childhoods is that neither of us remembers anything until about the age of five, and her very first memory is a sad one. I was born on September 21, 1936. Georgette tells me that on the day my mother came home from the hospital with me, I was placed in a bassinet at the foot of my mother's bed. When Georgette came in to see me, she leaned over to touch this new creature who was now her sister. Immediately, my mother scolded her, warning her in a very stern voice not to touch me. The way she said it, according to my sister, left Georgette fearful of ever touching me again.

Both my sister and I had fair skin and very blond hair, unusual features in the traditionally olive-skinned and brown- or black-haired Arab community. Georgette's hair was straight, mine was extremely curly. In my early childhood, my mother would create long sausage curls around her finger. Later on, she would use strips of rags to set my hair, trying to control it as it grew thick and bushy. Our traits were frequently remarked on, by both family members and friends. I have no idea where those characteristics came from, but from the reactions of my aunts and uncles, I knew they considered us special. Even to this day, I'm amused by people's reactions when I refer to my Middle Eastern background. It's as though what I've said about myself and what they had imagined about me are so different as to be irreconcilable. One day when the writer Alice Walker came into the studio on one of her many book tours, we began talking about my background. When I mentioned to her that both of my parents were Arabs, she laughed delightedly, and said, "Why Diane, all these years you've been 'passing'!"

My mother's education was limited to the ninth grade. She spoke fluent French and Arabic, but her English was what was once called "broken." That it was not perfect remained a source of embarrassment for her throughout her life. She rarely came to my schools for plays, musicals, or any of the other events when parents usually visited. Once, when a teacher called to ask her to accompany my third-grade class on a field trip, she complained at the last minute of a headache and stayed at home. It was the only time she ever came close to being a part of an official school function. My father, on the other hand, had completed high school and spoke perfect English.

The relationship between my mother and father was warm

and affectionate. It's difficult to recall a single moment of anger between them, which is not to say that there weren't disagreements. But the relationship between parents and children in our household was clearly defined. We were not to know anything of their adult world, and that included their disagreements. My sister has told me that life had not always been so placid between them. Uncle Toufic, with whom we shared a house, confided that in the early years of their marriage, my mother and father fought bitterly at times, hurling accusations and even throwing things at each other. But by the time I came along, things were quite different.

When my father returned from the store each day, his first question after opening the door was "Where's Mama?" If she was upstairs in her bedroom, or downstairs cooking, or out in the backyard, he went directly to see her, before taking off his hat or coat. It was as though he had to verify her presence each day, and after each parting. Conversely, I can't remember a time when she went out of the house if he was there, except, perhaps, for a brief walk. I can still see my father slipping up behind my mother as she stood at the kitchen sink doing dishes. He would put his arms around her waist and, believing perhaps that I couldn't see, put his hands gently over her breasts. She would laugh softly and tell him to move away. They slept in the same bed until my teenage years, when they finally brought twin beds into their bedroom.

He rose quite early in the morning, since he did the primary marketing for the store, and would be out of the house by 4:00 a.m. in order to find the best produce. On a few occasions during summer vacation from elementary school, I would get up and accompany him, feeling the excitement of riding in the truck with my father through the darkened streets of Washington, and being with him as he spoke to various suppliers about the choice fruits and vegetables at one of Washington's oldest and busiest wholesale markets. There were practically no women present, only men, all of whom had warm words and smiles for me. It was a market of strong smells, vivid colors, and loud voices, as produce bearers and buyers unloaded and loaded their trucks. I never strayed very far from my father's side in those vast stalls, always fearing that somehow I might lose him.

One of my strongest memories is of an incredibly well-stocked refrigerator, with every imaginable fresh fruit and vegetable. Coming home from school at the end of each day, I could look forward to peaches, plums, cherries, or apples, or perhaps a fresh ripe tomato that my mother had grown. Sitting down with a tomato or cucumber, saltshaker in hand, listening to one of my favorite late-afternoon radio programs, remains a delicious recollection of childhood. I'm fortunate that I never got into the habit of packaged snack foods such as potato chips or candy bars, but my sister and I simply never had the opportunity. On occasion, we were allowed cupcakes, or even a pie on Sundays, but only as a special treat.

I have little understanding of the power relationship between my parents. My father was thirteen years her senior, but I believe Mama exerted her influence whenever she needed to. I know he adored her, and wanted to do whatever she asked. What was absolutely clear was that their relationship was the most important one in the family; we as children were secondary. My parents' needs and wishes, especially my mother's, were paramount in the household, and my sister and I understood that very clearly.

The major source of puzzlement in my life is why my mother's relationship with my sister and me was so difficult. We've asked ourselves and each other, but neither of us understands. To the world, and to our aunts, uncles, and cousins, Mama was the lovely, warm, and gracious Eugenie. To us, she was a bitter, angry, depressed woman who had very little in the way of a positive emotional connection to us. Perhaps it was that my mother saw herself as "special," and yet, in this environment dominated by her sisters- and brothers-in-law, wasn't able to achieve the status she believed she deserved. Having two girls who were clearly doted on by relatives, friends, and teachers may have intensified her own feelings of separation and isolation from those she loved.

I grew up in what is now called the Petworth section of Washington, D.C., in the northwest part of the city. When I was young, our neighborhoods didn't have such clear delineations. Streets with names like Upshur, Varnum, Webster, Taylor, Randolph, and Shepherd were my landmarks. The houses bordering ours at 1429 Taylor Street, and on the streets around us, looked very much like each other: neat row houses with columned front porches. On summer evenings, we could see practically everyone in the neighborhood simply by walking out onto our cool, shaded front porch and gazing to the left or right. As kids, we played sidewalk games while our parents and grandparents sat, rocking and watching. It was a terrific location, within walking distance of my elementary, junior high, and high schools. I realize now just how richly diverse the neighborhood was, with families of Greek, Italian, Jewish, and Arab origin living side by side.

Rock Creek Park was just a short bike ride away. Riding down Taylor Street, turning left on Arkansas Avenue, and then coasting down the hill with my hands off the handlebars under the Sixteenth Street Bridge and into the park was pure joy. On hot summer days, the temperature seemed to drop dramatically once you were past the bridge. There were benches and picnic tables near the cool creek, where we took sandwiches and homemade lemonade for lunch. The traffic in those days was so light you rarely had to worry about a car coming up behind you or near you. On some days, a group of us would take hot dogs, start a fire in one of the stone fireplaces, and roast them on long sticks.

As an adult, I've passed the house on Taylor Street many times, and I can see how small it is. Back then, it didn't seem so.

There was a foyer leading to a center hall through an alcove to the kitchen. The living and dining rooms were off to the right, and off limits. A sliding glass door between the living and dining rooms was closed at all times, to discourage us from using that as a passage to the kitchen; in that way, according to my mother, we wouldn't wear a path in the living room rug. The kitchen was at the back of the house, adjacent to the den, which overlooked the backyard. Downstairs in the basement there was an extra stove, an extra refrigerator, and a washing machine. We didn't own an automatic dryer—clothes were either hung out to dry in the backyard or, if it happened to be a rainy day, on long lines that were strung the length of the basement. Before they were hung out, they had to pass through a wringer on the washing machine, a chore I sometimes shared with my mother. I can still see the two of us taking the dried sheets and towels off the lines and stretching them diagonally, from the corners, to return them to their rectangular shape. If the clothes had been hanging outside, the smell was divine, filled with sunshine and fresh air, a scent that no chemically bottled concoction could ever imitate.

On the second floor of our house, there were four bedrooms and a single bath, plus my mother's dressing room, which overlooked the garden. Our modest backyard was filled with fruit trees, rosebushes, and flowers, all the product of my mother's constant efforts. A fig tree, a small peach tree, and a cherry tree were lovingly cared for. The secret to perfect figs, according to my mother, was a daily dose of used coffee grinds at the roots, a task either my sister or I was called on to perform regularly. There was also a grapevine on the fence separating our property from our neighbor's, the source of delicious leaves that my mother would stuff and roll with lamb and rice and a topping of homemade yogurt.

My mother was a marvelous cook and seamstress, making most of my girlhood coats and dresses. One of my vivid memories of her dexterity with a needle is of watching her fashion a skirt for my sister, who'd just been elected to the cheerleading squad at Roosevelt High School. Georgette came home with a borrowed royal blue pleated skirt that all the girls were expected to wear with their thick white sweaters emblazoned with an *R* for Roosevelt as they performed their leaps and kicks. My mother took one look at it, opened up the large mahogany dining room table, created a newspaper pattern, and, in a couple of hours, managed to produce an exact duplicate to fit my sister. I watched her silently, never asking questions but realizing that something beautiful was happening. It was a talent I considered magical, and a gift I came to realize in later years that I had inherited from her.

I have only fragments of memories of my early childhood, prior to the age of about eight or nine. A special favorite: during the elementary grades, I came home from school for lunch each day. The aroma of lamb chops greeted me as I came onto the porch. It was the one time of the day when I was alone with my mother. I can see her moving about the kitchen as I sit down to eat. She would ask me about the morning's events at school and tell me what was expected of me later in the day. Afterward, I'd walk our brown and white fox terrier, Patsy, up to the corner and back. Then I was off to the afternoon session of school. At the end of the day, when I came home again, I would see my mother lying on a sofa in the den. She was weary and frequently complained of headaches. She didn't seem pleased to see me, and would urge me to change my clothes and go back out to the playground. These memories, however fragmented, are not easily shed.

I knew our family was "different," but I wasn't sure how. The very fact that my mother didn't seem as active or as involved in school matters as the parents of my friends was one difference, but there were others. There was a constant admonition "not to tell" anything about our family which made me uneasy, afraid that I would somehow say something I shouldn't say that would violate the rules as they were laid down. The very smells in our home seemed different from those of my friends'. That notion was reinforced when my mother would comment, after I'd been to someone else's house, "You smell just like them." Now, in my adulthood, I am all too sensitive to smells, especially coming from other people's clothing. Finally, there was the silence. When my friends came into our house, I inevitably had to "shush" them so they wouldn't disturb my mother. For that reason, it was always more of a treat for me to play outdoors or go to a friend's house than to invite someone to ours.

What I'm certain of is that my opinions were never invited. To question a decision made by my parents, or to protest any action of theirs, would have been unthinkable. I marveled at my peers, whose parents not only engaged them in conversation but seemed genuinely interested in what they had to say. Indeed, their parents also invited my comments on whatever they might be talking about. It was an extraordinary luxury to be heard, and even valued, for my thoughts and ideas. In this day and age of "kids first" and the concentration on developing a sense of esteem, it seems almost unbelievable that such an utter lack of encouragement and participation could have existed. But this was another era, a time when children were to be "seen and not heard." The extremes to which it was carried in my family, however, made it difficult for me to develop any kind of belief in myself or sense of self-confidence.

One of my favorite spots to explore in the house when no one else was at home was my mother's vanity table. It stood in a small dressing room separated from my parents' bedroom by glass doors. Made of burled walnut, it had a tall, oval central mirror and two smaller, movable side mirrors. There were drawers on either end, plus a central drawer, each holding a fascinating array of cosmetics: lipsticks, powders, rouge, hairpins, combs, and hairnets. The fragrance of powder, as well as Elizabeth Arden Bluegrass cologne (a scent I wear even today), filled the room.

There I could experiment with tiny dabs of lipstick and powder, or dot my cheeks with rouge, knowing full well I'd have to be ready to wash them off quickly if my mother returned home unexpectedly. Because it was exclusively hers, it was a room I never dared go into when my mother was in the house, but it seemed to contain the essence of who she was. Through the windows of her dressing room I could see our garden, and the garage opening onto an alleyway. The alleyway provided a shortcut to school, but as a child I was uncomfortable taking that route. The backs of houses seemed to me more mysterious than the fronts, and I felt insecure.

During the early part of my childhood, we shared our home with Uncle Toufic and his son, Sam. My aunt Maggie, Uncle Toufic's wife, had been placed in an institution here in Washington, St. Elizabeths. The diagnosis, as I learned later, was kleptomania. In addition, she'd suffered a stroke, leaving one side of her body so paralyzed that she dragged one leg and had to keep one arm from flopping by holding it against her body. She was a loving woman, and I looked forward to her infrequent visits. While everyone in the family treated her warmly when she came home, there seemed to be an unspoken agreement not to mention her name or her whereabouts at other times. After Sam married, he and his wife, Victoria, purchased a home of their own, and Uncle Toufic moved in with them.

On Sundays, before my family owned a car, my father would take me by bus down Sixteenth Street to visit his sisters. They all lived within a two-block area of Seventeenth Street, near P. Aunt Wadia and her husband, Uncle Jimmy, owned a small grocery store and lived in the apartment above it. Aunt Julia and her husband, Uncle Bill, owned a restaurant on the corner of Seventeenth and P. They, too, lived in the apartment above their eating establishment. Aunt Fahima and her husband, Uncle George, lived in an apartment just two doors away. It was always a treat to go from one aunt's to another's, knowing that I would be greeted by cousins delighted to see me, as well as delicious cooking smells coming from each of their kitchens. Aunt Wadia's and Aunt Julia's apartments seemed the noisiest and the most fun, because in each there were three or four children, all of whom teased me and brought out toys for me to play with. As we ran from one room to another, shouting with laughter, it seemed a far cry from our own subdued household. At home, my mother constantly admonished me for having too loud a voice. Here in my aunts' homes, there were no such restrictions, and we all seemed to laugh together.

For a long while, I was curious as to why my father's three sisters always seemed to be cooking the same meals for Sunday dinners. I thought it was some grand design they had, choosing to prepare and share the meals together. When I finally questioned one of the aunts about this, the answer was logical and reasonable: it depended on what was on sale at the Safeway. Whatever it was, they all bought and cooked the same thing!

My mother didn't accompany us on these Sunday visits; they were specifically a time for my father to be with his sisters and their families, and he seemed to enjoy himself immensely. I can see him sitting in each of their kitchens, smoking his cigarettes as they cooked and tried to tempt us to stay and share the meal. But my father wouldn't do that. Instead, we would leave at about noon, and our own Sunday dinners would take place later in the afternoon.

Summers afforded a chance for extended visits with aunts, uncles, and cousins, as Aunt Julia and Uncle Bill owned a home right on the shore at North Beach on the Chesapeake Bay. Occasionally, our family would go down to visit for an entire day, or even a few days, either to stay with Aunt Julia or to rent a cottage nearby. North Beach was, at the time, a small family beach, with lots of kids about, bingo parlors, penny arcades, slot machines, and fresh blue crabs. The entire family would sit at picnic tables with newspaper spread across them, feasting on crab meat. My belief at the time (and my husband's belief even now) was that one had to do an awful lot of work to enjoy one delectable morsel! Nevertheless, the memory is a happy one. My only sour recollection of those times has to do with being undressed in public, with my mother and aunts forming a circle around me on the beach. I can't have been more than six or seven, but my sense of being exposed left me angry and humiliated. I couldn't understand why I wasn't allowed to go into one of the changing rooms to put on my bathing suit. But my tears and protests were of no avail.

My cousins tell me I was a polite child, courteous and respectful. My own recollection is that I was probably somewhat spoiled by these aunts and uncles, who viewed me as a bright, attractive girl and allowed me liberties they might not have permitted their own children. But even as I enjoyed every minute of being with my relatives, I knew instinctively that our own family was somehow different. We lived in a house rather than an apartment. Our home was in a residential neighborhood on a tree-lined street, as opposed to a commercial one, filled with stores, restaurants, and traffic. Our living room had lovely draperies, slipcovered furniture, and handsome carpeting. The draperies and slipcovers had been sewn by my mother, and created a warmth and a softness I didn't find in the aunts' apartments. Even the smells, emanating as they did from a grocery store or restaurant below, were discernibly different from those I perceived in our own home. I could also see that my mother looked different from my aunts. She wore pretty clothes that flattered her figure, and the uncles enjoyed talking with her. There were many evenings when I'd find an uncle or two, plus several cousins, visiting our home, sitting and talking with Eugenie. My bedroom was just above the foyer, but close enough to the living room so that when we had company, I could put my ear to the bare floor and catch snatches of their conversation and laughter. Much of the time, they would speak in Arabic, telling each other stories and sharing family gossip. I never dared to ask a question about what I'd heard, however, since that would give away the fact that I'd been trying to listen through the floor.

I have no idea how much money my father earned as a partner in the grocery business. Nor do I have any sense of what his personal investments may have brought him. I do know that he was very active in the stock market, going first to the business section of the morning and evening newspapers to check on how his investments had fared that day. His mood would shift, depending on what he read. On at least two occasions, he visited the New York Stock Exchange, and was very excited by what he saw. My mother went with him once, but she had very little to say about the experience. Seeing the look on her face when they returned, I knew better than to ask any questions.

CHAPTER 3

OURS WAS A STRICT and orderly household, with regular daily chores assigned to both my sister and me. We made our beds, emptied trash cans, and cleaned bathrooms from a very early age. Promptness was taken for granted. If one of us was late coming home from school or, later, from a date, there was hell to pay. If some of our aunts or uncles were visiting, even a slightly raised eyebrow from my mother would indicate to me that I had said or done something to offend her, and was in big trouble.

Both my mother and father believed in, and practiced, punishment, both physical and psychological, a fact that leaves me with many painful memories. It doesn't help to realize that, at least in those days, corporal punishment was a common means of enforcing discipline. What I do know is that when I was slapped in the face or beaten with a belt, a metal pancake turner, a large wooden spoon, or a hard-soled shoe, I couldn't avoid the blows.

It's strange that I didn't defend myself, and I wonder about that even now. Why didn't I run? Presumably, I knew that if I did, the punishment would be even worse.

One day in particular stands out in my mind, when I was about eight. I was spending the morning with a friend next door, the wife of a U.S. Army colonel, who was teaching me to embroider. A classmate was with me, a friend my mother wasn't particularly fond of. I was due home at twelve-thirty for lunch, but I'd become so involved with the embroidery lesson that the deadline passed. The phone rang and my classmate reached for it. I was aghast when I heard her say, "Oh yes, Mrs. Aed, Diane's already gone home." I grabbed my belongings and rushed out the door, knowing that my mother would realize my friend had lied. As I ran into the house, my mother was waiting at the front door for me, a look of fury on her face and a metal pancake turner in her hand. She began beating me, her rage beyond anything I'd ever experienced, so terrifying that I crumpled to the floor, trying to hold on to myself, hoping she'd stop. But the beating intensified as she struck blow after blow to my head, shoulders, and arms, to the point where, out of fear, I lost control of my bladder. It's a moment that makes me cringe even as I recall it more than fifty years later.

I'll never be convinced that hitting a child is a useful form of discipline. Perhaps it temporarily relieves a parent's tension, but it does nothing to instill respect. Fear, yes; respect, no. Indeed, those beatings instilled in me a sense of shame. It was a secret I kept, somehow believing I deserved to be treated badly because I'd disappointed my parents. I saw their anger with me as justified, no matter how extreme. There was no way to separate myself from my feelings of self-hatred for having behaved so badly. It was impossible for me to blame them for their loss of control.

The beatings also left me uncertain about what to expect from my parents. There were days when the mood seemed pleasant and I felt safe. There were days when I would congratulate myself on having been a "good girl." But then came the moments when my mother's rage would descend and I didn't know where to turn or how to run. If the dishes weren't dried or I'd accidentally torn a piece of clothing or had uttered some word of frustration, I knew instinctively that I was in for it. Even as I write this, I experience the confusion I felt as a child. It took many years of therapy to begin undoing the harm those beatings inflicted on me.

Another form of punishment my mother exercised was withdrawal. After a physical beating came the almost more painful experience of being shut out. No matter how I tried to win her affection, there might be weeks when she would ignore me. A direct question elicited no response. It was as though I was invisible. In extreme cases, I was confined to my room, and not permitted to play with friends after school. The confinement did not allow privacy, however, since neither my sister nor I was permitted to close our bedroom doors.

That memory came back to haunt me when, in their early adolescence, first our son, David, and then our daughter, Jennie, insisted on closing their bedroom doors, appropriately claiming their privacy. Jennie went so far as to put a large KEEP OUT sign on her doorknob. Initially, I raised strong objections, insisting that there would be no closed doors, but my husband stood firm in defense of their right to choose a closed-door policy. It took weeks for me to settle down and understand my own anger and opposition to their freedom. Without even knowing where it was coming from, I was foisting on them the same restrictions that had been placed on me.

My father was less inclined toward the "silent" form of punishment. With smiles and quiet gestures, he would somehow manage to let me know that eventually the clouds would lift. Because of his somewhat more lenient attitude, it was hard for me to understand his role in the physical punishment. There were times when my mother would wait until he came home from the grocery store and then demand that he beat me for some infraction that had taken place earlier in the day. I had the feeling he did so somewhat reluctantly, but he did it nevertheless. My belief is that he wouldn't have been inclined to physically hurt either of us had it not been for my mother's insistence.

That my parents imposed such strict discipline has seemed, in many ways, the central fact of my childhood. The sense of obedience and order was very deep and, I daresay, stifling. My mother suffered from headaches, insomnia, and other mysterious ailments throughout my childhood. The long periods of silence that were so characteristic of our household seemed to come from a desire to make life as peaceful for her as possible. The effort to maintain it, however, came at a price. Friends of mine who were invited to our home to play had to be chosen carefully for their soft voices and willingness to engage in quiet games. I experienced painful stomachaches for which there seemed to be no relief, but I never told my parents about them, fearing I would somehow be punished, forced to miss school, or denied the opportunity to be outdoors with friends. At times I hid myself beneath the dining room table, lying flat on my stomach over a dining room chair, hoping to ease the pain. Or I would go for a walk, breathing deeply, looking up at the sky, hoping the fresh air and sunshine would reduce the discomfort. These episodes lasted into adulthood, when, thanks to John Rehm, I began to face the underlying tension triggering the problem. Years of therapy, plus a radical change in diet, helped the situation immensely. Even now, though, my stomach is an accurate gauge of what's happening in my head. When the tension rises, the discomfort begins.

In contrast, some of the happiest moments of my childhood spent with my mother are centered on the radio. Those were the days of "The Lux Radio Theater," "The Green Hornet," "The Shadow," "The Greatest Story Ever Told," "Stella Dallas," and many other outstanding radio dramas. If my behavior was deemed deserving, I would be allowed to listen to "Lux Theater" in my parents' bed, often curled up next to my mother under a satin comforter. The fragrance of Bluegrass was always in the room and on her person. The two of us shared the pleasure of listening to other daily broadcasts in our small den, curled up together on a small sofa. Saturday mornings, after I'd finished my chores, brought the high point of the week. This was the weekly broadcast of "Let's Pretend," in which fairy tales came to life through the voices of gifted actors accompanied by extraordinary sound effects. I have since purchased some of those old radio programs on tape, and listen to them occasionally on long trips, and I continue to be amazed at the images created by that small group of actors and the sounds that enhanced their voices.

One might have thought that because of this separation between my parents and their children, my sister and I would have developed a close bond. Instead, what existed between us was a deep strain that could be overcome only for very brief periods of time. We were constantly at odds, but we carried out our disagreements in private. Our parents rarely saw us argue because we both knew that arguments would create a terrible uproar and might actually bring on a beating for both of us. Therefore, our fights—and they were very physical—took place only when our parents were not in the house. I can recall hiding the backs of my hands and arms from view because they were covered with scratch and bite marks left from our altercations. I'm sure I gave as good as I got, but we tend to remember only our own wounds.

This relationship of mutual distrust and even dislike between Georgette and me lasted throughout our childhood, adolescence, teenage years, and into early adulthood. It was difficult to bring ourselves to get beyond the underlying insecurity we both felt, fearing as we did that the next day, or the next minute, would find us defending ourselves against an onslaught of parental rage. Instead of comforting each other, we deflected our personal pain and anguish by turning against each other. Even now, with both parents long dead, it hasn't been easy for us to find a way to talk openly with each other about our shared life. We've tried, on more than one occasion, to bridge the gap between us. In the past few years we've both worked at the relationship more diligently and, I believe, more successfully. We phone each other more frequently and spend more time talking than we've done in prior years. It thrills me to hear her say to me "I love you," and to say the same to her.

Some years ago, at a dinner celebrating Georgette's birthday, I began to talk with her about my memories of growing up in our home, and the bitterness I felt at our parents' (particularly our mother's) inability to do anything other than lash out in anger when something we did displeased her. I spoke of the beatings, the feelings of shame and worthlessness that had encumbered me since childhood. My husband had heard these stories, and he sat by quietly. But Georgette seemed stunned, and stared at me as though I had lost my mind. She told me she had no such recollections and had simply put our childhood behind her. As I sat there listening to her denial, I felt hurt, angry, and finally, saddened. I knew I hadn't imagined the events as I had related them to her, and it was clear she had suppressed comparable memories. It wasn't until nearly six months later, at Christmas, that Georgette told me she knew that my recollections were real and that she had spent her whole life pretending to herself that none of it had ever happened. When I had raised the subject on her birthday, she said, she wasn't prepared to deal with it, but later, in quiet remembering, it had all come back to her, filling her with an anger that she had long denied existed. That conversation went a long way toward repairing the rift between us. Perhaps we finally recognized that we had lived through a deeply traumatic childhood and shared a common enemy, and that we didn't need to continue allowing that enemy to divide us.

My father smoked Pall Mall cigarettes, using a black cigarette holder, which always embarrassed me. I wondered why he couldn't just smoke cigarettes the way my friends' fathers did, without that long extension protruding from his lips. Even seeing an occasional photograph of President Roosevelt with a similar apparatus didn't impress me. My father smoked a lot, even though he suffered from high blood pressure, and even after his heart attack in 1948. At that point in our history, there were apparently no studies warning of the link between smoking and health. Even if there had been, I doubt that he, or any of his brothers, would have given up such a deeply ingrained habit.

My father walked with a distinct limp, the origin of which I was not to discover until many years later. Even to describe it as a limp is not quite accurate. It was a rolling shuffle, one he said he feared would someday cause him trouble with the police, who might mistake it for a sign of public drunkenness. Thinking back, it is hard to understand how he could have served in the U.S. Army during World War I with this affliction, so it must have come on later. The effort involved in walking for more than a block or two created severe discomfort for him. The older he got, the worse it got. His sisters—the twins Fahima and Wadia, as well as Julia—also had the problem, whereas neither of his brothers, Toufic and George, was afflicted. Wadia gave birth to twins, Alice and Louis, both of whom suffered the same deformity, as did Fahima's son, George, and Julia's son, Henry.

In the summer of 1960, shortly after John and I were married, and when I was in my sixth month of pregnancy, the National Institutes of Health began a study of Charcot-Marie-Tooth syndrome, named for the French Canadian physicians who discovered the genetic origin of the problem. I, along with many of my cousins, some of whom had experienced walking abnormalities and some of whom had not, were asked to come to NIH to participate in the study. I was, of course, particularly interested in whether I might be a carrier of the gene, and whether the child I was carrying might be born with the same inherited trait. I was assured that the tests I would undergo would in no way harm our child. As it turned out, the examination consisted of filling out many forms detailing our physical history, plus undergoing some physical tests. My sister and I were among the lucky ones who had no trace of the problem. The genetic disorder, passed through the women in my father's family, created a shortened heel tendon, which meant that walking became concentrated on the front part of the foot and the toes, preventing the heel from touching the ground first. It affected other muscles in the legs as well, tightening them and creating pain that my father lived with for all of his life. It saddens me that I came to a full understanding of my father's difficulty only after his death.

CHAPTER 4

*M*Y EARLY YEARS of school mark the clearest beginnings of my childhood memory. I was so incredibly proud to skip up to the top of Taylor Street where it intersected with Fourteenth, go left down the hill to Upshur Street, and cross Fourteenth with the Patrol Boys. They were much older, of course, fifth and sixth graders who'd gone through special training to assist younger children in crossing those streets. There were also D.C. police stationed at some of those busier intersections, officers I came to recognize and respect, and who I knew were watching over my classmates and me.

From the earliest days of kindergarten, I knew I was in my element. I can still see those small chairs in the first classroom on the left at William B. Powell Elementary School, a cheery classroom with colorful cutouts all around. Our teacher (whose name I can't recall, though I do remember Mrs. Houston in first grade and Miss Morris in second) was a small woman with bright eyes and curly hair who showered warmth and affection on all of us. I'm certain it was those very characteristics that allowed me to step outside my "home" boundaries and express myself joyfully and even exuberantly at school. It was in kindergarten that my love of playacting began, with a starring role as the witch in *Hansel and Gretel*. Our staging area in the classroom was appropriately set apart from that of the audience, with plenty of room for cardboard props to indicate a forest and a small cottage. I stalked and talked and crouched with sufficiently convincing menace that my teacher encouraged me to appear in a number of other "productions" that year, all of which were performed for the entire school body. It was the beginning of a lifelong love of drama, affording me the opportunity to appear regularly in plays put on by the school and our local recreation center. I've always wondered why these early experiences didn't frighten me. To the contrary, they seemed quite easy and natural. Memorizing lines was never a burden because I could do it without a huge expenditure of effort. Perhaps performing was a way of moving outside myself and my environment into a world I found more comfortable, accepting, and even exciting.

School became my place of freedom. I was a bright student, eager and willing. Throughout elementary school, learning was a joy. Each new English grammar, arithmetic, science, history, or geography assignment was carried out with gusto. I knew my teachers were fond of me, and I was eager to please them. One in particular, Mrs. Houston, lived close by, and I would visit her on my way to or from Sunday school. That I could enjoy a personal relationship with an adult not related to me was very special. She never failed to send me home with fresh pears from the tree in her garden, pears that I found delicious, though my mother would remark that they were "very green."

Though my parents were part of the Christian Arab community, they rarely attended Sunday services. They did, however, baptize both my sister and me at St. George's Syrian Orthodox

Church in Washington. I began attending Sunday school and
singing in the children's choir at Hamline Methodist Church at
Sixteenth and Allison Streets NW, primarily because a few of my
friends in the neighborhood went there. It was within walking
distance of our house, but often the parents of one of my friends
would give a group of us a ride.

My love of music began with those early days of Sunday
school and singing in the children's choir. The choirmaster and
organist was Mrs. Rawls, whose rule was that we had to attend
Saturday rehearsals or we would not be permitted to sing on
Sunday mornings. I loved the rehearsals because she was such a
gentle teacher, helping us to learn to hear ourselves as individuals
and the blending of our voices into a chorus. I watched her fingers as they moved across the keys of both the piano and the
organ, marveling at how effortlessly she played. Then, on Sunday mornings, after Sunday school lessons, I felt proud to put on
a long dark robe with a white collar and a large bow that Mrs.
Rawls tied for me and proceed ahead of the adult choir down the
center aisle as the organ played. Adults stood in the pews, singing
loudly and smiling down at us as we moved toward the choir loft
behind the pulpit.

One Sunday morning in particular stands out in my mind.
When my friends and I arrived at church and went to our classes,
instead of the usual bright and cheerful atmosphere, there was a
strange hush in the room. Before the morning ended, we all
learned that the mother of one of our classmates had hanged herself, and that her child, Miriam, had found her. It was the first
time I realized that a mother could be so unhappy as to remove
herself from the world.

God became a very important figure in my life, starting with
those early days at Sunday school. I prayed to Him easily and frequently, asking Him to help make me a good girl so that my
mother wouldn't be so angry with me. I loved to listen to the sto-

ries of Jesus, to picture Him as a young boy, amazing the elders. I felt His kindness and His watchfulness over me. I could see Him and imagine that He regarded me as a special child, even though He could not protect me from my mother's rage. When I found myself alone in my room, I would get down on my knees and pray for His help, believing that He would show me the way. I had no difficulty sincerely believing in His ability to perform miracles.

One occasion underscored that for me. One Christmas, my parents and Uncle Toufic gave me a gold stretch-band bracelet with a heart in the center, something I had seen in a jewelry store on one of my fairly frequent walks between our home and the Tivoli Theatre at Fourteenth and Park Road. I had told them about it, and had actually pointed it out to my mother on one of our walks to the movie theater. When I found it under the Christmas tree, I was overjoyed. It was the most beautiful treasure I had ever owned. When I returned to school after the Christmas vacation, I proudly showed it to my friends. But then one day, to my horror, I couldn't find it. I knew I'd had it on when I left the house, and I recalled taking it off briefly during a playground recess. And then it disappeared. I was beside myself. Not only had I lost this most precious gift that I loved, but I knew my mother would ask about it and discover that I had lost it. I had no idea how she would react. Throughout the rest of the day, I prayed, again and again, that somehow, somewhere, I would find my bracelet. I began looking around at other girls' jewelry, suspicious that somehow it had been stolen from me. I was afraid to go home.

Finally, the awful hour of three o'clock came and I knew I had no choice but to go. I tried to think of how I could tell my mother the truth so that she wouldn't be furious with me. I begged God to help me. I counted every single crack in the sidewalk, trying to calm my heart and my stomach, which felt as though it was going to overflow. When I got home, my mother was lying down. I went straight to see her, not yet having gathered the courage to blurt out the truth. Slowly, I walked up the stairs to my bedroom to change my clothes. And there, in the center of my bed, lay the bracelet.

To this day, no rational explanation will account for its reappearance. I was convinced that I had left the house that morning with the bracelet on my wrist. I had, of course, made my bed before I went to school, and it certainly was nowhere to be seen at that point. Later, I asked my mother whether she had put the bracelet on my bed. She said no and, fortunately, didn't ask any questions about it. There's a part of me that will always believe that, just maybe, a miracle occurred.

My parents expected me to do well in school, and expressed no surprise at the periodic report cards indicating that my work was "outstanding." That was the designation used in those days. There were just three possibilities on those elementary school reports: OP (for outstanding progress), SP (for satisfactory progress), and U (for unsatisfactory). They would smile and nod approvingly, the only indication that they were proud of me. What seems surprising to me now, as I look back, is that there wasn't a single book in the house other than the King James Version of the Holy Bible, which my mother read often. No one ever gave me a book, and I never purchased a book. The only books I read were those assigned to us in school. Other than those, I don't believe I ever read a book on my own until I became an adult. There were numerous magazines—*Good Housekeeping*, *Ladies' Home Journal*, and *Life*—but those were primarily for my parents. I went to the public library on very rare occasions. Though it was only a few blocks away, I felt intimidated by the huge stacks and had no understanding of how to go about finding a particular book. It was a major gap in my childhood learning. Yet despite the lack of reading material at home, I was deemed an outstanding reader and was frequently called on to read to the entire elementary school body. I feel pride in those memories, and saddened at how much more I might have been able to learn had there been more encouragement from my parents.

At least twice a year, D.C. police and firemen would visit our school, inspiring both respect and awe. They walked and spoke with such authority, while reminding us that they were our friends. I can still sing a song the D.C. chief of police taught us when I was in first grade. It went something like this:

Remember your name and address . . . and telephone number,
    too.
Then if someday you lose your way, you'll know just what
    to do. . . .
Walk up to that kind policeman, the very first one you
    meet . . .
Then he'll be kind and help you find your house on your very
    own street.

Today as I glance out my fourth-floor window on Brandy-wine Street overlooking Wilson High School, I realize that many students in D.C. public schools and around the country are without regular teachers, books, and even classrooms. Teachers are forced to deal with problems like overcrowding, gangs, guns, and drugs, which fifty years ago couldn't have been imagined. Instead of going through childhood and adolescence with a focus on education, many young girls today become sexually active and experience motherhood in their early teen years. Every week, there are newspaper and television accounts of violence in the schools, with gang wars and attacks on teachers and students.

In contrast, my childhood was spent in a world where teachers, policemen, firemen, doctors, lawyers, judges, and members of Congress were held in high esteem. My father spoke admiringly of the professional people with whom he came into contact at the grocery store. There were no polls equating levels of professional standing with public mistrust. In our young minds, we assumed that everything we had was the best because, after all, we lived in the best country in the world. That kind of patriotism and belief in America's institutions is something I grew up with, and still cling to.

The other source of freedom was the corner playground, Twin Oaks, at Fourteenth and Taylor Streets. When I was between the ages of about six and twelve, Twin Oaks was the center of my nonacademic learning. Boys and girls of all ages, scholastic and athletic abilities, from every neighboring community, gathered at Twin Oaks. We came together to organize softball, kickball, and basketball teams. We learned what good sportsmanship was all about. On summer nights, we watched outdoor evening movies provided by the D.C. Department of Recreation. We walked to the drugstore for ice cream. We played hearts and gin rummy. We painted pictures. We took pride in doing our part in keeping the playground orderly, with balls, bats, and nets collected and accounted for. And we followed the leadership of the playground director, Mrs. McGhee, a warm and loving woman who treated us all as though we were part of her extended family. When I think of all the families today who have to spend so much time carpooling kids to various athletic and extracurricular events, I look back on that era and realize just how fortunate we were. Ours was very much a middle-class neighborhood, but our riches seemed abundant. If my home life held terror, my external world was filled with many friends and caring adults. Luckily, I couldn't suspect that as I moved into early adolescence, that sense of security and stability would begin to disappear.

CHAPTER 5

*A*T THE AGE of nine, I experienced something that terrified me and intensified my anxiety about my parents' lack of regard for me. A lazy, peaceful summer afternoon was interrupted by the screaming and clanging of fire engines. A group of us raced from the playground to follow them as news spread that there was a fire in the neighborhood. As we stood at the corner of Arkansas Avenue and Upshur Street, watching in awe as the firemen unloaded their hoses and other paraphernalia, a well-dressed gentleman who was standing nearby struck up a conversation with me, eliciting my opinion on what was happening and how serious the problem was. He seemed genuinely interested in what I had to say. Since I was in the midst of a group of my friends, I felt no unease.

The next day, my mother received a phone call from the man who had been standing near me at the fire. He identified himself to her as a member of Congress and went on to say that he had met me at the fire the previous day, was extremely impressed by my childhood beauty and intelligence, and would very much like to take my parents and me to lunch the following week. My parents reported very little of this conversation to me, except to say that he had expressed his belief that I had the makings of a child film star. He could, he said, provide the guidance and wherewithal to see to it that this happened. My mother agreed to talk about it with my father, and then a decision would be made. I have no idea what kind of discussion took place between my parents. Perhaps because they knew how much I enjoyed appearing in school and playground theatrical performances, they assumed I'd be interested, but they never asked directly whether this was something I'd like to do. As for the fact that the man was a total stranger, I can only surmise that they were impressed by his social and political standing and were prepared to believe he would actually do as he promised.

Several days later, I was told we were going to a well-known downtown hotel for lunch with the congressman. He told my parents the hotel was his Washington residence, while his family stayed behind in his home state. My hair was neatly braided, my clothes pressed, and off we went. I had never eaten at a restaurant before, much less entered a hotel. I remember sitting rather uncomfortably in the dining room as the congressman talked with my parents about me and his plans for me. A waiter served our lunch and, much to my irritation, began to cut up my food for me. I tried to protest, but, from the look on my mother's face, knew I should be quiet.

The talk centered on the congressman's desire that I go to live with him and his family (he said he had a wife and two young girls, about my age) so that I could be educated and trained and groomed for a film career. In a day and age when young girls like Margaret O'Brien, Natalie Wood, and Elizabeth Taylor were becoming huge attractions, I can understand my parents' fascination with the possibilities. What I cannot understand is what happened next.

At the end of lunch, his proposal having intrigued my parents, the congressman told them he would like to buy me a piece of jewelry. He suggested that my mother and father return home and that he would bring me along shortly. They agreed, even as I tried in vain to signal my discomfort. I watched them drive off, with this stranger holding my hand. The congressman then hailed a cab and took me to a downtown jeweler, where he purchased two items for me: a three-monkey pin, representing the see-no-evil, hear-no-evil, speak-no-evil admonition, and a small sapphire and gold birthstone ring. When we got into another taxi, I assumed we were going directly to my home. Instead, he said he'd like to drop back at the hotel for something he had forgotten. I can remember feeling a rising sickness in my stomach, but I didn't protest for fear of offending him. When we arrived at the hotel, he took me through the lobby, into the elevator, and up to his room. He unlocked the door and asked me to come in. As soon as we were inside, he closed and locked the door behind us.

Having never been in a hotel room before, I had no way of gauging whether it was small or large. It seemed roomy enough to hold a large bed, which is about all I can remember. But what happened next remains extraordinarily vivid in my mind. The congressman removed his jacket and sat down on the side of the bed. He then patted the space next to him and asked me to come and sit by his side. I asked him when we would be leaving to return to my home, and he assured me we would leave in just a few minutes, so I did as I was told, moving to his side. He then took me in his arms, laid me down facing him on the bed, and began rubbing his hands over my legs and buttocks, kissing my face as he did so. He held me gently, but I felt fear in a way I never had before. I couldn't stand the smell of him, or the feel of his hands on my body. His cheek felt rough against my face.

Instinctively, I knew that what he was doing was wrong. Though my father, uncles, and cousins frequently kissed me on the cheek and patted me on the bottom, this was different. This strange man was doing something I did not want him to do. With some effort, I managed to move away from him, pushing against his chest and up from the bed. I walked straight to the door of the room, unlocked it, and opened it. I said to him, "I want to go home now." There was a look of amusement and even surprise on his face. He paused for a moment and then got up to put on his jacket. I stood at the open door as he did so. In a soft voice I shall never forget, he said, "You really are a smart girl, aren't you?" I didn't answer, but preceded him down the corridor to the elevator.

During the cab ride home, he talked more about how much I would enjoy living with his family, being with his children, and going to a school in his community. He was sure I would make a wonderful child actress. I listened to all this in silence, feeling my skin crawl with the memory of his hands on my body, loathing the sound of his voice yet knowing that I had to hold in my emotions until I was safely home. I said nothing and just gazed out the window, grateful for the presence of the taxi driver as we drove up Sixteenth Street to my home.

The instant the taxi arrived at our home, while he paid the driver, I jumped out ahead of him and ran into the house, yelling for my mother. She was down in the basement, cooking. I ran down the stairs two at a time, and when I saw her I screamed, "I hate him! I hate him!" In just a few seconds, I told her what had happened—how he'd taken me to his room, laid me on the bed, and touched me, and that I never, ever wanted to have to be with him again.

She looked at me in silence and then called to my sister, who was upstairs. She told her to take me out the back door, through the alley, and up to the playground, and not to breathe a word to anyone about what had happened. Georgette and I did just that, even as curious friends of ours came over to the table at the playground to ask why I was crying and what was wrong. My sister held my hand as I told her everything that had transpired, a moment that underscored, in my young mind, the seriousness of what had just happened to me.

I have no certainty about what words were exchanged between my mother and father, and, ultimately, the congressman. I only know that I was told I must never speak about the event—with anyone. The problem with that admonition was that it applied to our entire household. It was as though the experience had never taken place. I knew I wanted to talk about it— to ask my parents why they had left me, to tell them how frightened I had been, to ask why they had believed this man. I wanted to talk with someone, but I couldn't. I did learn later from my sister, who had apparently been told by either my mother or my father, that by the time the congressman came into the house from the taxi, my mother had already related to both Uncle Toufic and my father what I had told her. They became enraged and quite physical with the congressman. My uncle began to choke the man, threatening both to expose him and to kill him if he ever came near me again. According to my sister, the congressman got down on his knees and begged them not to divulge the story to the press.

For the rest of my adolescence and throughout my teenage years, I never got onto a streetcar or bus, or went anywhere by myself, without fearing that I would see his face. I was afraid he would find me and that somehow I would be forced to go with him. I never spoke about the experience again until after I was married.

I have since addressed those awful memories in various therapy situations, but I can never erase them completely. In fact, not more than two years ago, the anger I felt at being deserted by

my parents bubbled up at a dinner I was having with three
women who worked with me, all producers of "The Diane
Rehm Show" at the time. One of them mentioned that her
fourteen-year-old daughter had been invited to go to her boyfriend's house for an evening, even though his parents wouldn't
be there. My friend said she was inclined to allow her to do that
because she felt her daughter could handle herself well enough if
the situation were to become uncomfortable. Without realizing
what was happening to me, I found my voice rising and my heart
pounding as I began to accuse her of not exercising good judgment on her daughter's behalf. It was clear from the look on her
face that my reaction had stunned her; she had no idea why I was
reacting so strongly. She, as well as the other two women, became
very quiet, and finally one of them changed the subject. It wasn't
until we had left the restaurant and were standing in the park-
ing lot that I finally realized why I had become so upset. My
memories of that awful afternoon have left me with a wound
that will probably never heal completely. I apologized to my
three friends, explaining why I had become so emotional, and
in so doing realized once again how vivid that experience was
and is.

A postscript: I talked with my sister recently about the incident with the congressman, and she told me something I had
never heard before. Our mother gave her the monkey pin and
the birthstone ring, in their original boxes, and instructed her to
take the streetcar downtown and return them to the jewelry
store where they had been purchased. Georgette told me she had
exchanged the two pieces and received a fountain pen in return.

CHAPTER 6

ONE OF THE HIGH POINTS of my early adolescence was my grandmother's yearlong visit. My father had arranged for my mother's mother to come from Alexandria, Egypt, to be with us. She was a wonderful, warm, loving woman, but she spoke no English, so during that period I was forced to speak to her in Arabic. It was not a difficult transition for me, since my parents spoke to me in Arabic most of the time and I knew most of the vocabulary I needed to carry on a conversation with her. I remember rising early on summer mornings just to sit with her on our front porch, to rock and laugh softly and talk, and watch her smoke her cigarettes. Occasionally, she would allow me a puff (I was probably no more than eleven at the time) because she could see how curious I was about cigarettes. Her long black hair, which she wore in a bun during the day, hung loose on those mornings. I can recall asking her whether I might stroke it, because, even at the age of seventy-five, she had shiny, beautiful hair, without a trace of gray. It felt like pure silk.

While Taita (the Arabic word for grandmother) was with us, my mother was a happier woman. The entire atmosphere was different. She and my mother cooked, sewed, cleaned, and laughed together. The beatings stopped completely, perhaps due to my mother's discomfort at having her mother witness her violent behavior. On one occasion, however, when it looked as though my mother was about to lose control and hit me, my grandmother stepped in front of me and challenged her. My mother began to laugh uncomfortably, suggesting she hadn't really intended to inflict physical punishment. When Taita left at the end of her year's stay, I found my mother crying in her room. When I asked her what was the matter, she said to me, "I know I will never see my mother again." She was right.

When I was twelve, the world changed. My father, at the age of fifty-four, suffered a heart attack. The house, if it had been quiet in earlier days, now seemed silent. Since my father could no longer manage the stairs to the second floor, the dining room, where so much sewing had gone on previously, now became the sickroom. We were all very hushed in those days, and heavy with uncertainty about the future. There were murmurs of concern, and secretive conversations between my mother and my uncles. It was hard to understand what was happening. But after several months of convalescence, it became clear that my father would no longer be able to share in the operation of the grocery store.

Many months of recuperation passed before my father was able to leave his bed in the dining room. But slowly he mended, and finally could use the stairs once again. Working in the store, however, was out of the question. I overheard only snatches of conversation about money, but I understood that there was very little for anything other than necessities. To this day, I have no knowledge of where the money came from to support our family during that period. I knew only that my father could no longer provide a regular income for us from the store's earnings. In my childish outlook, he was diminished. It was during this period that I began to entertain fantasies that my Uncle Toufic, always solicitous of my mother, was actually in love with her and that he would be the one to keep us safe.

Actually, it was my mother who began to earn money to help meet the family's needs. For the first time in her married life (I have no idea whether she had worked before her marriage to my father), she went to work. I sensed it was a great embarrassment for her. When aunts or friends called, I was never to say she had gone to work, only that she was out of the house. Somehow, she managed to overcome her reserve and get a job at the Hecht Company Department Store, first in alterations, later in the monogram department. With her ability to wield a sewing machine, she quickly learned the techniques necessary and became one of their valued employees. My father and I would drive downtown to Seventh and F Streets NW to pick her up each day at 6:00 p.m.

My sister carried her share of the load by working at our local library. I was given the entire responsibility for cleaning the house, ironing, and starting dinner. At twelve, I became, for the first time in my life, a latchkey child.

In order to help pay the bills, my parents also took in two boarders, Mr. and Mrs. Hishmeh, for whom our basement was converted into a bedroom and kitchen. There was a half bath on that level, along with stationary washtubs. Their presence added to the sense of disruption and unease throughout our household. No longer did our home feel as though it belonged exclusively to us. Occasionally, when I came home from school, Mr. Hishmeh would be there by himself, and I would immediately retreat to my own bedroom on the second floor, fearing that I might have to make contact with him. My mother often complained about the smells of Mrs. Hishmeh's cooking, so different were they from her own. To me, Mrs. Hishmeh seemed like a very gentle

and quiet woman, tiny in stature and overwhelmed by her physically obese husband, who did most of the talking. After about
two years of living with us, Mrs. Hishmeh became pregnant.
Before the baby was born, they moved to another household.

    This was also a period of major transition for me, from ele-
mentary to junior high school. No longer was I in a single classroom with a beloved teacher throughout the day. I now had to
make my way from classroom to classroom and teacher to
teacher, in a far more complicated and demanding system. My
fear of getting lost, which I had felt steadily since my earliest
days, reduced me to a state of constant worry: I was never sure I
could find my way through the halls of the school, and still imagined that the congressman might be waiting in one of those dark
corners. My grades, consistently at the top of the class in elementary school, began to slip. I became familiar with the fear of
walking into a classroom without a grasp of the material we
were studying.

    That sense of self-doubt remained with me, but through con-
versations with my girlhood chums, I came to realize that what I
was feeling was not so different from what they were feeling. We
were able to share our anxiety about school, grades, boys, and
popularity in such a way as to make the burden seem somewhat
easier. Most of my childhood girlfriends shared my love of athletics. We spent many hours laughing together as we played softball, basketball, and tennis. Then we would manage to continue
the giggling and gossip over the day's events on the telephone
after school. I managed to squeeze in those phone calls even as I
did my required after-school chores around the house. However,
the sense of inferiority that emerged in those years of adolescence
has remained with me ever since, leading me to prepare almost
excessively for each day's radio program so that I can avoid the
feeling of sickness in my stomach.

    I had my first real "date" in ninth grade. Up until that time,
the boys and girls were always in groups, going to the movies

(our primary weekend pastime), sitting at the neighborhood drugstore soda fountain enjoying a sundae, or having a great time at the playground. So when I was invited by one of the junior high school's football stars to attend an evening picnic being given by one of my classmates, I was both excited and scared. Would he hold my hand? Would he put his arm around me? Would he try to kiss me? If he did, what would I do? Parents were present, of course, as we all went into Rock Creek Park for a cookout. When the young man arrived to pick me up, my mother stayed out of sight. But my father, adopting a very stern pose, grilled him on exactly where we'd be and what time I would be returning home. As it has been for generations and I'm sure always will be, it was a most uncomfortable and embarrassing moment, and yet I knew my father meant well.

As it turned out, it was a wonderful event, with perhaps six couples roasting hot dogs and marshmallows. We sang songs, told funny stories, and shyly related to one another. As I recall, there was no "making out," but there were lots of sweet glances and touches. Engaging in real sexual activity would have been out of the question, at least in my mind, in that day and age. The young man brought me home on time, and my father was waiting for me at the door. I don't recall having had other real "dates" in junior high school. It wasn't until I arrived at Roosevelt Senior High that my real social life began.

CHAPTER 7

SORORITY LIFE WAS an important part of high
school in those years. I was particularly keen to join one,
but at first my mother said absolutely not. Then my sister
stepped in on my behalf. She hadn't been allowed to join a sorority five years earlier, but she convinced my mother that if she
hadn't been a cheerleader, her social life in high school would
have been absolutely nil. Surprisingly, my mother relented and
allowed me to pledge to Omega Phi. There was a gentle hazing
period during which those of us who had been invited to pledge
had to undergo six weeks as "goats"—that is, the lowest of the
low. We were not permitted to wear lipstick, and had to curtsy
each time we saw one of the members of the sorority, with our
index finger beneath our chin. All this had to be done in secret,
because sororities were not allowed by the school. The rules were
not strictly enforced, however, and I'm certain the administra-
tors knew full well of the existence of such groups.

After completing the six-week goating period, we had to undergo a "hell" night in which we were razzed and taunted and forced to carry out silly, but never dangerous, tasks, such as wearing foolish clothing and makeup, begging on the streets, or being led blindfolded into semiscary situations. But once all that was behind us, we had great times together. Weekly Friday night meetings were held at the homes or apartments of each member, with tuna sandwiches, potato chips, Cokes, and cookies. After the meetings ended, the boys would be allowed to drop in for some talk and dancing to the favorite popular songs of the day, sung by Frank Sinatra, Perry Como, Joni James, Peggy Lee, or Nat King Cole. I felt fortunate to "belong," to be part of a group of girls who sat together at lunch and at sports events, or met to gossip with each other after school. Belonging provided me with a feeling of security, so much so that I confess I gave little or no thought to those girls who didn't belong in the same way.

As a teenager and throughout my life, I was highly critical of my looks. Every time I looked in the mirror, I hated seeing my reflected image, despite the fact that friends would tell me how pretty I was, how good my hair looked, or how clear my skin was. I knew I was one of the fortunate ones in that regard, because I never suffered from that teenage dread, acne, but every girl I looked at seemed prettier, smarter, funnier, or more popular than I. Comparing myself with others was a habit I fell into. Of course, this was a time when how you looked was very important. Neatness and cleanliness were assumed. Our clothes were washed and ironed. Most of us wore white socks and saddle oxfords, white with brown or black trim. It was a nuisance to keep them clean, but an important part of the entire "look." At one point during that high school period, I was asked to pose for a local newspaper wearing what was deemed the "appropriate" apparel of the day.

One memorable moment contributed to my lack of confidence about my looks. I served as a bridesmaid at a cousin's wedding, perhaps the only time in my teenage years when my mother attended an event where I wore a gown and had flowers in my hair. As I stood next to her, feeling pride in the moment, a gentleman whose name I didn't know walked up and said, "You have a beautiful daughter, Mrs. Aed." My mother responded without hesitation, "No, she's not beautiful. You might say she's pretty, but she's not beautiful." I had no reason to question her conclusion, but I was crushed to hear her utter those words aloud so firmly.

My first "steady" boyfriend was a young man named George Murray, who was the pitcher for Roosevelt's baseball team. He was also an outstanding piano player. As I recall, our relationship began with the usual teasing and playfulness. At the time, I never thought of what we did as "flirting," but I'm sure that's what it was called. George and I shared several classes, and he would catch my eye from time to time. Then he invited me to go with him to a basketball game, and from then on we were a couple. He was a sweet young man whose good manners and clean-cut presence seemed to please my mother and father. They had no complaints about him, and didn't seem to mind his being around the house. I remember feeling relatively comfortable with him, trusting that he would never do anything to hurt me. But that didn't mean I trusted him completely.

The episode with the congressman had definitely affected my attitude about boys, so that I was wary and watchful, particularly in those early days of dating. Though there were times when our relationship became intensely physical, with lots of kissing and petting, the thought never occurred to me to "go all the way." The opportunities for mischief were there, however. George and I would meet after school, at the home of one of my dearest friends, Lynne Benton. Her mother and father were divorced and her mother worked on Capitol Hill, so Lynne's house was empty in the afternoons. Lynne and her boyfriend, Bobby Miller, and George and I took advantage of those moments.

Why didn't we engage in sexual intercourse, considering that we were alone in that house? First of all, the sexual act sounded pretty bizarre to me, even in high school. There was no such thing as true "sex education" in those days, except for physical education classes just for girls which explained menstruation. I had virtually no understanding of how the sex act "worked," or why two people would want to do something that, from my vantage point, sounded pretty uncomfortable and extremely intimate. To my mind, the sexual act, whatever it consisted of, was strictly reserved for marriage, despite the fact that there was one young woman in our class who had to leave school because she was pregnant. We all felt sorry and embarrassed for her, but for me, coming from a family like mine, there was absolutely no doubt about what was right and what was wrong. There was no effort on George's part to try to pressure me or change my mind, and for that I was grateful. Our relationship lasted for a little more than a year, until I met a handsome lifeguard at one of the swimming pools I frequented during the summer.

Neil Leary was about six feet six inches tall, a basketball player and about to be a freshman at Shepherd College in West Virginia. I found him enormously attractive, but because he was a bit older than I (and presumably more experienced), I responded to him cautiously, not allowing myself to spend long hours alone with him. My mother liked him and saw him as a sweet giant. His intensity about the relationship began to trouble me, however, as he talked about his plans for our future together, and I found myself making excuses as to why I couldn't see him.

My interest in him subsided as I became increasingly attracted to Bill Roberts, a young man who had suffered from spinal meningitis two years earlier. As a result, he had lost a year of schooling, as well as the hearing in one ear. Had the illness not occurred, he would have graduated a year ahead of me, with a mediocre scholastic record, but after his illness he became a much more serious scholar and was well liked and respected by

all of our classmates as someone who got along well with teachers and students alike. We dated from the latter part of our
junior year until we graduated.

In that same junior year of high school, my father informed
me that we were moving to a house on Riggs Road, in northeast
Washington. I have no idea what influenced my parents' decision to leave our home and move across town, to a house that had
very little charm and was located on a busy street. My parents
had always said how much they loved the quiet of Taylor Street.
Perhaps, after the Hishmehs moved out, the house on Taylor
Street had become too expensive and they could no longer afford
it. At about the same time, an unbelievable blow fell. At sixteen, I
learned that my mother was dying.

CHAPTER 8

*N*O MATTER HOW SICK or tired she'd been for all the years of my childhood, it never dawned on me that my mother could actually be seriously ill. As a child, I had no way of comprehending the talk, the whispers, the worried looks that surrounded us all. But when I was sixteen, afflicted with an abscessed ear, I was taken to see our family doctor. My father went into the doctor's office first and, as I sat in the waiting room, talked with him for perhaps twenty minutes. When he came out, my father indicated he'd wait for me in the car.

I was uneasy at the thought of being alone with the doctor (fear of being alone with any grown man other than my immediate relatives had become part of my behavior pattern), but I did as I was told. The doctor looked at my ear and pronounced it to be definitely abscessed. At this point, he took a cotton-swabbed stick and poked it in my ear, breaking the abscess, which nearly sent me screaming out the door. But instead I sat there crying. He told me what I was to do to care for it, and gave me some medications to use. Then, as I rose to leave, I got up the courage to ask, "Doctor, how is my mother?" And in precisely the same manner he had used when cleansing the abscess, the doctor said, "Your mother is dying. She has cirrhosis of the liver." I found the voice to ask how long he expected she would live. He said possibly eighteen months to two years. And with those words, he ushered me out of his office.

I went out to the car in a daze, not believing what I'd heard and at the same time understanding that it must be true. When I got to the car, I knew for certain. For the first time in my life, I saw my father weeping. He pulled himself together and told me that I mustn't let my mother know what the doctor had told me because that would make matters worse. He said we must all do everything we could to keep Mama happy, and that we must never say anything at all about her illness.

So, in the belief that denial is a way to postpone reality, there was no discussion of my mother's illness. By this time, my sister had married, and she and I talked almost not at all. Even later, when my mother went to the hospital for lengthy stays, there was no acknowledgment that she was suffering from a terminal illness. I continued high school, confiding to few friends about my mother's condition. Aunts, uncles, cousins, and friends visited the house, ever solicitous of my mother, who always smiled and said she was feeling just fine. The priest from St. George's Syrian Orthodox Church made numerous visits as well. Whenever he was present, my mother would direct me to kiss his ring, an act that made me seriously uncomfortable.

Despite her illness, life went on as it always had. My father confided that money was very tight, especially with my mother's medical bills, so I got a Saturday job at the Hecht Company doing filing in the credit department. Though the pay was low, it gave me spending money to buy clothes and school necessities.

Throughout high school, my parents stressed the importance of learning typing and shorthand. They expected me to go to work as a secretary immediately after graduation, and honing those skills seemed the surefire way to accomplish that. College was absolutely out of the question, not only because there was no money available but because college seemed to my parents without value. It's important to note, however, that some of my male cousins—sons of my father's sister Victoria—had attended college and medical school. One became a physician, the other a dentist. My mother loved those young men, and her face shone with pride when she spoke of their accomplishments.

In my parents' defense, I didn't see myself going on to college, either. Part of me couldn't have imagined leaving home at that time, and the thought of four more years of schooling had no appeal, though perhaps as many as half of my classmates were college-bound. Until just a few months before graduation, I didn't think very much about college at all. By the early spring of 1954, with graduation coming up in June, something happened inside me, making me wonder whether I could possibly spend the rest of my life going to work as a secretary each day. When I finally approached my mother to ask her, however haltingly, whether there was any possibility I might be able to attend a local college such as the University of Maryland, she made it very clear, not surprisingly, that it was out of the question.

I graduated from high school in June of that year, at age seventeen, with my parents and Aunt Wadia in attendance. My mother had by this time been admitted to Georgetown University Hospital several times, but between those stays she seemed to manage fairly well. As for my own future, it seemed clear: I would go to work as a secretary. By this time, I was seeing Bill Roberts exclusively. He was voted president of the graduating class; I was cochairman of the senior prom; and together we were named "Cutest Couple" of the class. It was clear, however, that our relationship would soon come to an end, since he planned to go on to college. I envied him, and knew that it was hopeless to believe that once he had an opportunity to experience a university atmosphere with all its variety, he would want to maintain our relationship. But despite that separation and the breakup of our high school romance, we've remained good friends throughout the years. When he and his wife have visited here in Washington from time to time, it's always fun to remember those days with him.

Immediately following graduation, I went to work for the director of the D.C. Highways Department, J. N. Robertson. I worked as the assistant to his secretary, took dictation from her and him, and was given various typing assignments. One of the most enjoyable aspects of the job was that I became the radio voice to the Highways Department workforce. It was a very simple system, a two-way radio in our office which reached the supervisors out on the streets. Mr. Robertson would instruct me to get on the radio to inform a crew about a particular pothole or any other kind of repair work necessary, or call for a crew to be reassigned. I had great fun talking with the men on the various crews, and they came to know my voice. I lived at home, handing over half my salary to my mother and dad for room and board.

It was during this period that the final physical confrontation occurred between my mother and me. Something I did one Saturday morning displeased her, and in less than a split second I could see the fury move across her face as she raised her hand to slap me. For the first and only time in my life, I raised my arm to protect myself and said to her, "Mama, that's enough. Don't ever hit me again." She looked at me, absolutely stunned. She stood staring at me for a moment, her eyes filled with loathing, and then turned and walked away, saying something to the effect that I was worthless and had been disrespectful toward her.

A year later, I was offered as a promotion a position with the U.S. Postal Inspection Service, where I worked with inspectors investigating cases involving use of the mails for illegal purposes.

Moving from road repair to mail fraud was particularly interesting for me, as it showed me a very different side of the world from any I had seen before. Cases involved small-time swindlers trying to use the mails to misrepresent their products, as well as big-time con artists creating networks of illegal operations. I listened with fascination as various inspectors dictated their reports.

My social life was definitely on the wane after the camaraderie of high school. Gone were the daily conversations with close friends, the sorority parties, the football and basketball games. So, with my parents' encouragement, I became increasingly involved with members of the young Arab community in Washington. There was a sizable group of men and women, all somewhat older than I, who attended the Syrian Antiochian Orthodox church and were part of a young adult social group. Together, we enjoyed picnics, beach outings, baseball games, and visits to local restaurants. I loved being part of the group. On chartered buses we'd head for the beach, singing all the way. Many of us loved to sing so we harmonized on our favorite songs.

It's interesting to recall that in those days, men and women were seated on opposite sides of the Orthodox church. We were not allowed to sit together. I was taught early on that I was not to cross my legs in church but to sit with both feet on the floor. Another admonition: a woman was not allowed to attend service if she was menstruating, the idea being that we were unclean. The service was in Arabic, much of the music was sung by a chanter, and I understood none of it. The entire ritual felt so very different from that which I had experienced growing up in the Methodist church, with its colorful stained-glass windows, the glorious organ music, the congregational singing, and the beautiful solos. I also felt somewhat out of place because of my blond hair. Many people commented on it and asked me about it. There were very few people my own age. Before long, I found myself increasingly involved with George Hamaty, a man eight years my senior. George had been in the army, stationed in Japan, and seemed extraordinarily worldly and sophisticated. He was also a man who loved art, and had produced several canvases of his own. He was a master of the Arabic dance, gracefully moving his body to the sounds of the oud and special drums. He offered to drive me to various social meetings, invited me to dinners and dances, escorted me to church, and, in the spring of 1955, proposed marriage. I was eighteen years old.

It was clear by this time that my mother's illness was worsening. Her retention of fluid made it seem that this always slim woman was now eight months pregnant. Nevertheless, there was no outright conversation about it, with one exception. On a day when she and I were at home alone, my mother came to me with several pieces of her precious jewelry in hand. Very seriously, she said, "Diane, I want to talk with you about my bracelets and rings, and my lavaliere." I looked at her and saw the tears in her eyes, and I couldn't bear it. I said, "Mama, why are you doing this? We don't need to talk about this. This jewelry is yours and always will be!" On the verge of breaking down, she said, "You have to let me talk about this. No one will listen to me! I *have* to talk about it!" Without waiting for further reaction from me, she held up her two braided gold bracelets. I knew them well because she wore them daily, having brought them with her from Egypt. She said one was for me and the other for Georgette. She also said she wanted me to have a very unusual reversible ring with a raised cameo on one side and a black onyx nightingale on the other. It was something I'd tried on in secret for many years, never once imagining it would come to me in this way. And finally, she gave me her small, delicate lavaliere with a tiny diamond in its center. She put the three pieces in my hand, closed my fingers over them, and left the room.

There was a great deal of conversation about George Hamaty, and what a good family he came from. People have asked me whether my parents pressured me to marry George. The answer is, outwardly, no. There was never a word spoken to indicate that this was what they wanted. What I did know, however, was that they were pleased with him—that there was nothing I could do that would please my mother more than to marry him. When George asked my father for my hand in marriage, my father was delighted.

George and I planned a large church wedding to include much of the Arab community, to be held on January 7, 1956. In late September 1955, however, shortly after my nineteenth birthday, my mother was again hospitalized, this time for a week. It was during this period that I had an opportunity to talk with one of her doctors, and I told him that George and I were to be married in January. He looked at me very carefully and said, "If I were you, I think I'd move that date forward a bit." At first, I couldn't comprehend what he was telling me, but as the shock wore off, I realized he'd finally uttered the awful truth: my mother would be dead within a few months.

George and I hurriedly rearranged our plans, setting a new date for October 16. Instead of a large church wedding, it would be for just the two immediate families and take place in our living room. The only additional person was an old family friend, Harry Hier, who had performed with Borah Minevitch and the Harmonica Rascals, who played "Here Comes the Bride" as I came down the stairs. As the Syrian Orthodox priest stood with us to perform the ceremony, including the traditional exchange of crowns, my mother lay on the sofa in the living room, dressed in her navy blue quilted housecoat. The photographs of that day show a smiling groom and guests, and a very serious bride.

George and I rented a newly constructed apartment just five minutes away from my parents' home, but it wouldn't be ready for us until January 1. My parents were pleased to have us live with them for the brief period, especially since this meant we could keep my father company during my mother's now extended hospitalizations. During the period leading up to Christmas, I spent time with her, alone in her hospital room, not really talking, just sitting by her bed. Occasionally, I would put my head down on the bed near her hand and she would stroke my head. The Syrian Orthodox choir came to Georgetown Hospital to sing carols for her and other patients on Christmas Eve. Both she and my father stood in the hall together, listening to the music. It was the only time I ever saw the two of them cry together. The next day, I came to the hospital alone to bring her a Christmas gift, a Hummel figurine to add to her already substantial collection. She had always loved the sweet faces and delicate carving, so I assumed she'd be pleased. Instead, when she opened it, she said to me, "Why did you do this? Why did you spend your money on this?" It was an excruciating moment for me because, since I could not accept the idea that she was going to die, the gift made perfect sense. She lay back on her pillow and turned her face away from me.

On New Year's Eve, 1955, George and I spent the day moving into our new apartment. All the furniture we had purchased, plus the rugs and draperies, had been put in place, and now we were finally setting up an independent household. The telephone wouldn't be installed until the day after New Year's. By the time we'd finished getting the apartment into livable condition, it was nearly 10:00 p.m., which left us just enough time to swing by the hospital.

We got to Georgetown at about eleven, and when I went in to see her, my mother was sleeping. Not wanting to wake her, George and I started to leave the hospital, and on our way out we ran into the doctor who had earlier advised us to move up our wedding date. He asked whether I had spoken to my mother. I answered that we had been in to see her, but that she was asleep and that I didn't want to wake her. To my surprise, he urged me to go back into her room and make sure she knew I was there. I again expressed my reluctance, citing her difficulties with insomnia, but he convinced me that I should waken her and speak with her, if only briefly. So George and I went back into her room, and I was able to rouse her. I wished her a Happy New Year and then lowered the sidebar on the bed to kiss her. I told her I loved her. Groggily, she waved me away. Her words still wound as I replay them in my mind. "Go on, girl," she said. That was the last time I saw her alive.

As I look back on that night, I'm sure the physician who urged me to see her knew that her life was ebbing away, and that there was a good chance she wouldn't live through the night. I'm glad he convinced me, but saddened that I didn't spend more time with her. I think even then I was in denial that the end was near, choosing to believe that there would be other opportunities to talk with her and to be with her. Instead, we went to a New Year's Eve party, though neither George nor I was in a partying mood.

On New Year's Day, we slept late, arose around eleven, and began working around the apartment. At 2:00 p.m., there was a loud knock on the door. Somehow, I knew before I opened it that there was something terribly wrong. It was George's brother, Nick, who had raced across town to our apartment to tell us that we should go to the hospital immediately; since the telephone wasn't yet installed, he had no choice but to come directly to our apartment. We ran to Nick's car, and he broke all speed limits driving to Georgetown Hospital. When we arrived, I raced ahead of both men to my mother's room, but it was too late. She had died twenty minutes before we arrived. My father, my sister, my uncles, and several aunts were in the room. My mother was still propped up in her bed, dressed in the same navy blue quilted housecoat she'd worn on the day I was married.

As sick as I knew her to be, I hadn't really accepted the idea that she would die. I had just pushed it out of my mind, refusing to understand or appreciate that she would be gone. I knelt at her bed and sobbed, crying not only because she was dead but also because I felt guilty that her death brought me a sense of relief. I knew she would never beat me again. My sister knelt with me, and as I touched my mother's hand and stroked her yellowed skin, I realized that the warmth of life had not completely left her body, and that if only I had been able to get to the hospital a little sooner, perhaps she would have said good-bye.

Of course, there is much about my relationship with my mother that haunts me. Most of all, I believed that she could read my mind, that she could see directly through my forehead into the inner folds of my brain. That left me at a loss, because not only would I not have dared to say anything to her that might be considered disrespectful, I couldn't even allow myself to think those thoughts. Nevertheless, there were times when I did, even going so far as to wish her dead. It was awful to have such thoughts, to try to hide them, even from myself, and to fear that somehow she might know that they were lurking in my mind. But the fact is, they were. To know that and to accept that about myself is very hard.

What was the explanation for her death from cirrhosis of the liver? We will never know for certain, but it's been suggested that it was related to the malaria she had suffered as a young woman, before she came to this country. The pattern of alcoholism usually associated with cirrhosis did not apply to her. She and my father enjoyed a single shot of whiskey together on Thanksgiving, Christmas, and New Year's Eve; other than at those times, I never saw her take a drink. The doctors at Georgetown who treated her were very skeptical at first, but eventually realized that she was telling the truth.

My grandmother was never told of her daughter's death. The reason the knowledge was withheld, I was told, was that she was in poor health, and to learn that her daughter had died would have been too much of a blow. But she must have known. My mother wrote frequent letters to her in her beautiful Arabic handwriting. I would see my mother writing and ask her what she was telling her mother, but she never shared that with me. My father never read the letters, either, since my mother would address and stamp them and I would mail them. Once the letters stopped, my grandmother would have to have realized that her beloved Eugenie was gone.

After my mother's death, my father seemed like a lost soul. My sister, her husband, and their two children moved out of their apartment and into the house with him. I know he valued their companionship, but at the same time he had great difficulty adjusting to the noise and activity of a young family. He had begun driving a taxi in Washington a couple of years earlier, to keep himself occupied and to earn some money. Now the hours he spent in the taxi and away from home lengthened. Often, he came to our apartment, hoping I might cook dinner for him and allow him to nap in quiet. And then, one Sunday evening in November 1956, just eleven months after my mother's death, while George and I were bowling with friends, Papa had another heart attack.

When we arrived at the Veterans Hospital on Wisconsin Avenue (now the site of the Russian Embassy complex), the doctors assured us that my father's condition was not life-threatening. We saw him briefly, but they then urged us to go home, promising to call if his condition changed. Before we left his bedside, my father said to my husband, "George, take good care of her." When he said those words, I realized he thought he was dying. Since the doctors had assured us that he would be fine, I kissed him and told him we'd see him first thing in the morning. But it was not to be. At about 2:00 a.m., the call came, urging us to return to the hospital. By the time we got there, he was dead. While the official cause of death may have been a heart attack, I knew in my own mind that my father had died of a broken heart. He had no desire to live after Eugenie's death and was, I believe, ready to give up this earthly life in the hope of joining her. As if to confirm that belief, several days after his death I saw him in a dream hanging by a rope from the ceiling in the center of my living room.

My father's funeral, like my mother's, was an awful affair. Neither my sister nor I had much to say about the arrangements, but those two funerals shaped my own view of what I would never want for myself. Both caskets were open, surrounded by flowers that filled the room. The embalmed bodies within bore almost no resemblance to the parents I had known, loved, and feared all of my life. By the time my father died, I felt emotionally empty, not at all sure I could make it through yet another two-day wake and a funeral. But finally it was over. I can remember riding away from the cemetery where my father was buried next to my mother, sitting in a limousine with my aunt Annette, Uncle George's wife. She opened the window and cried out, "Take him, Eugenie. He's yours." Though I was embarrassed by her emotional outburst, I thought at the time that her assessment of the situation was absolutely correct.

Looking back, it's hard to grasp just how devastating their deaths were. Together, they were such an overwhelming presence in my life that I could hardly imagine making a major decision without them. But I did go on, knowing I could never fully put my family experience completely out of my mind. It's who I am and how I came to be. It wasn't what I'd like it to have been, but there are aspects of it that at some level have strengthened me and given me the courage to persevere. I've had to learn to live with my fears. Reaching that point has taken many years. I've created a life for myself that is very different from what it would have been had they lived. What I could never have foreseen was just how different it would be.

CHAPTER 9

*T*HROUGHOUT THE difficult period of my mother's illness and death, followed by my father's death, George and I became increasingly distant. I felt very little warmth or affection for him. I was grieving for my mother, but I had no desire to be comforted by him. My father's death intensified my lack of ability to reach out to George. I turned away from him, rarely wanting to be in his company.

I came to realize that George had married me expecting that our life together would be the same kind of life he had had with his family. He had been well cared for by his mother, who did his washing and ironing for him, cooked and cleaned for him, did whatever errands needed to be done, and asked very little of him in return. After all, I had come from a background very much like his, where my father's every domestic need was catered to. There were times when both my parents would be seated in the den and my father would ask her to get up to get him a glass of

water, which she did without protest. The memory did not sit
well with me.

Somewhere deep inside me, despite my mother's example, I
believed that the responsibility for a household should be shared.
I earned at least as much money as George did at the time. I came
home from work just as weary as he was. It wasn't as though I
had free time to do the grocery shopping, the laundry, the cooking, and the cleaning. Yet he expected all this of me, because that
was the way he had been brought up. For the three years we
were together, the lack of equality in the division of chores was a
sore spot that generated endless hostility between us. Now, forty
years later, I know that many women have had those same feelings, but in that era few of us expressed them.

By this time, George and his cousin, Lew White, had purchased a small dry cleaning store not far from our home. His
hours were long, and he worked six days a week. We both left for
work early in the day, and I usually arrived home by six in
the evening. He closed the shop at seven. When he came in, I had
already prepared dinner, and we sat down together. I would ask
him questions about the business, how it was going, about his
customers and various problems he and Lew were facing. I
would also try to talk with him about my experiences at work,
but the responses he gave were so minimal that I soon gave up
trying.

After dinner, George would leave the table, lie down on the
living room sofa, and fall asleep while I washed and dried the
dishes. Cleaning up the kitchen was a job I had never minded,
but I would have liked to have had some company as I did it.
Then I would read for a while or watch a television program
while he went on dozing. When it was time for bed, he would
wake up, come to our bedroom, and begin to make amorous
advances. By that point, though, I was simply not interested. I
didn't feel I had a true partner. I resented his unwillingness to

share the household obligations. I rebelled at the lack of communication between us. And most of all, I hated the silence.

Our lives at the time seemed almost exclusively framed by the Arab community connected to the church, and while I loved the people within that community, I yearned to know others whose views were different, and to have other experiences. I dreamed of buying a home in a distant area, of establishing a life apart from the church. I wanted to grow and to learn more about the world, but defining "more" was impossible. I only knew that my discontent was enormous, and that each day in the marriage had come to represent a stifling of my very existence as a human being. In short, I think the death of my parents unleashed in me a desire that had lain deep within me for many years.

I began to talk of separation, at first only in anger and then later in quiet seriousness. In the beginning, I don't think George believed I would do anything so foolish as to leave him. He seemed to dismiss my threats as though he were reacting to the pouting of a child. After all, there had never been a divorce in the Arab community; it was truly unthinkable. But by this time I had gone to work as a secretary at the Department of State and had been exposed to people whose views of life were far broader than those of our immediate friends and relatives. I had actually been recruited by the State Department through one of our Arab friends, who knew of a secretarial job opening and approached me about it. The move from the Postal Inspection Service to State afforded me both a higher salary and a fresh outlook on the world at large and my own world in particular.

In November 1958, two years after my father's death, after many long discussions that usually deteriorated into arguments, I asked George to move out of our apartment. I felt sad for him because it was clear that separation was not what he wanted. Yet even as I was filled with anxiety for him and for myself, I knew it was the right decision. Just to ensure that I wouldn't change my mind at the last moment, I asked a friend to come and stay with me as George packed his bags and left the apartment. And then, at last, I was on my own.

I realize now that had my parents lived I could never have made the break. It simply would not have been possible, because it would have brought shame on them and they would have done everything in their power to see to it that I continued in the marriage. But their deaths, as devastating as they were, liberated me from the confinement of family and community. I also knew in my heart that had we had children, the outcome might have been very different. But there were no children, and so for the first time in my twenty-one-year-old life, I was finally free to make a major decision for myself.

CHAPTER 10

L IVING IN AN APARTMENT alone was both freeing and frightening. In all my life I had never spent a
night by myself. There was never a time when I'd
awakened without knowing that someone who knew me or
cared about me was nearby. It was a very strange but somehow
exhilarating feeling. I felt cut off from the Arab community,
knowing that my actions had hurt friends and relatives alike.
Thanksgiving and Christmas were hard to get through that
year. I deliberately slept late on both of those days, to minimize
the feelings of loneliness and isolation.

Slowly, gradually, I began to make new friends among the
women at the State Department. Since athletics had always been
an important part of my life, when I learned that the State Department was recruiting for a women's softball team, I was eager to
become part of it. There I met women who were interesting and
fun to be with, and who shared my love of sports. The softball

team played in a league composed of other government agencies, with some pretty impressive players. The camaraderie was terrific, and a way to begin creating a new social life for myself. I've kept in touch with many of those women over the years, one of whom, Rozanne Ridgway, the catcher on our team, rose in the Foreign Service ranks to serve as the U.S. ambassador to East Germany before the Berlin Wall came down.

It was primarily through my association with those women that I began to be invited to various parties and dinners, but at least for the moment, I wasn't seriously interested in dating any one man. I did change one important aspect of my life: I moved out of the apartment I had shared with George and into a new one on New Hampshire Avenue in Foggy Bottom, just a few blocks from the State Department. In May 1959, after we had been separated for seven months, George and I were divorced. There was no resistance from him, only a feeling of profound sadness.

My secretarial position at the Department of State was in the Office of African Affairs, working for the political/economic adviser, George Dolgin. It was through George that a brilliant, talented, and brash young lawyer named John Rehm entered my life. George had begun working with John on a particular foreign aid issue, and raved to me about what a fine mind this young man had, and how mature he was beyond his twenty-eight years. The first time I met John Rehm, however, my own impression of him was decidedly different. When George introduced us, I was taken aback by John's loud voice and teasing manner, which seemed almost rude to me. He seemed so confident and had such a playful manner that I found myself feeling very uneasy. I learned later that his background was very different from my own, with an emphasis on education and learning, and with two parents who had adored their only child.

John was born in Paris to American parents. At the time,

his father, George Rehm, was sports editor of the Paris *Herald-Tribune*. His mother, Mary, who was the product of a very proper Philadelphia upbringing, had gone to Paris in around 1922. At five feet ten, weighing about 120 pounds, and with bright red hair, she was a natural for the couturier salons and worked as a runway model. The two of them met at a Paris gathering and were married in 1928. When John was born, on November 23, 1930, so the story goes, there were a number of reporters on the *Tribune* staff whose wives were pregnant. As the only male born to the group, John was immediately given the nickname "Scoop."

The family stayed in Paris for six years, returning to this country in the summer of 1937. George made the decision to leave because he believed Germany was going to invade France in the near future. They had very little money at the time and settled in Lynbrook, New York, in a house owned by Mary's sister. George took several positions and finally landed a job as the foreign publicity manager of the 1939–40 New York World's Fair. He then went to the Office of War Information in New York, serving on the French desk. In the late fall of 1942, he went overseas with OWI and was responsible for setting up radio stations and beaming U.S. propaganda in North Africa, Sicily, Italy, and southern France, areas occupied by the U.S. Army. In the meantime, John's mother moved into an apartment in New York City, leaving John in the care of a stranger, a woman he called "Aunt Katinka." Though John came to love Aunt Katinka, who looked after him with warmth and affection, it was during that year that his stomach began to give him problems that have lasted a lifetime. I've asked John how he felt at that point, with his father leaving for Europe and his mother depositing him in the care of a stranger for nearly a year. Like most children, however, he simply accepted the situation. In 1943, he moved to New York to be with his mother and was enrolled on scholarship at Friends Seminary, a private school in Manhattan.

One year after the end of World War II, in November 1946, John and his mother sailed to France to be with George in Marseilles, where he served as head of the United States Information Service bureau for that part of France. John attended a French high school during that year, studying primarily French literature and Latin. In 1947, Truman's "do-nothing" Republican Congress so severely slashed the appropriation for USIS that they closed down a number of bureaus, including the one in Marseilles, and that summer the family returned to the United States.

For quite a while, George had been considering the idea of buying a farm somewhere in the Northeast, and in the fall of 1947, after touring parts of New Jersey, New York, and Pennsylvania, he settled on a 155-acre working dairy farm in northeast Pennsylvania. Meanwhile, John returned to Friends Seminary to finish his senior year and then won a scholarship to Harvard. He completed a double major in Latin and Greek, and upon graduation, to his parents' astonishment, he decided on law school and received a scholarship to Columbia Law School. After graduation, he went to work as an associate with the Wall Street firm of Willkie, Farr, Gallagher & Walton. But at the end of one year, he decided that a Wall Street practice did not satisfy him, so when he was offered a position in the Department of State's Legal Advisor's Office to join a small unit specializing in the foreign aid program, he moved to Washington.

In those early days of coming to know John, I gradually overcame my initial impression and began to realize what an interesting man he was. I was also aware that he was an avid baseball fan—he, too, played softball for the Department of State, on the men's team, of course. So little by little, as we shared our interests in the office, our relationship began to expand, first to the softball fields, and then to dinners, movies, art galleries, concerts, long walks in the parks, and wonderful conversations. John would stand in line early on Monday mornings for tickets to the Friday night Library of Congress concert series (at the time, they cost twenty-five cents apiece), featuring the Budapest and Juilliard string quartets. Those concerts were a first for me, and I felt intimidated sitting in that audience of music lovers, listening to the extraordinary performances, while John was totally enraptured. But his excitement about the music was infectious, and as he expressed his ideas on what we'd heard, I found myself understanding and appreciating the music more fully.

John also introduced me to my first art gallery, the Phillips Collection. It was the perfect introduction because the gallery is a private home, lending the entire experience of viewing the art an intimacy that I wouldn't have experienced in a large museum. John felt particularly close to the Phillips because its founder, Duncan Phillips, had been a supporter of John's uncle by marriage, the painter Arthur Dove. At a time when Dove and his wife, John's aunt, Helen Torr, had almost no money and were struggling to survive, Phillips bought his works, which have long been featured at the Phillips.

John loved working in the kitchen and knew far more about cooking than I did. Cooking became one of many satisfying activities we did together, and I learned a lot from him. I appreciated the fact that whenever we prepared supper together, we cleaned up together. I had never been with a man who interested me as much as John Rehm did. He represented a different world, one I'd never before encountered, characterized by education, sophistication, and a sense of ease with oneself and others. Even now, I remain amazed at his range of knowledge and awareness of subjects that I've barely heard about. I've often thought he would make a wonderful talk-show host, with his warm manner and broad base of understanding.

Before long, John bought a small secondhand car so that we could take drives out to the country together. I still remember those warm days filled with sunshine in September 1959 when we took picnic lunches out into the rural areas of Montgomery County, Maryland. On one particularly brilliant Saturday afternoon, John spotted a haystack and couldn't resist stopping the car, climbing over the fence onto some unsuspecting farmer's private property, climbing up the haystack, and sliding down. The trouble was that beneath the dry surface, the stacked hay was wet, leaving a rather dark stain on his light khaki trousers.

When he proposed to me at the beginning of December, it was actually the second time he'd popped the question. The first had been three weeks earlier, in the course of a romantic dinner, with soft lights and music in the background, at a restaurant on Seventeenth Street in downtown Washington. By that time, we'd been seeing each other for nearly a year. I had come to know and love his energy, his enthusiasm, his strength, his honesty, and his intellect. I had some concerns about his occasional withdrawal, moments when he seemed distant, hard to reach, and uncommunicative, but I attributed this behavior mostly to the tremendous burden of responsibility he bore at the State Department. He worked long hours and was attracting the attention of numerous senior department officials.

When, on that evening, he began to talk about marriage, I was thrilled. To my recollection, we made tentative plans and talked of various possibilities for the wedding. We both agreed that a large event wouldn't be possible (neither of us made a lot of money at the time) or desirable (because as far as the Syrian Orthodox church was concerned, even though a divorce had been finalized, I was still married to George Hamaty). As I left him that night to return to my apartment, I was less concerned with those details than I was excited about the prospect of spending our lives together. But the very next day, to my horror, John said he had no recollection of having asked me to marry him! I couldn't believe my ears, and more to the point, I didn't want to. I felt a mixture of outrage, hurt, and humiliation, believing that somehow he had made a fool of me. So I did what my instinct told me was the only thing to do: I said I never wanted to see him again.

For three weeks, I went out of my way to avoid him. When I heard his voice in the hallway near my office, I slipped out another door. When I saw him walking in the street, I turned and went the other way. It was a very tense time for me and I was miserable, but I knew I had no other choice but to make a clean break. On the third weekend after the breakup, an old high school friend invited me to come to Virginia to stay with her for a few days since her husband was out of town, so off I went, trying to put what I thought by then was a broken romance completely out of my mind. When I returned to my apartment that Sunday evening, I asked the woman at the switchboard whether I'd had any messages. "Nothing much to speak of," she said. I asked what she meant. "Well," she said, "no messages other than that male friend of yours came by." Just to make sure we were talking about the same person, I asked whether she meant John Rehm. She said yes, that's exactly who she meant. It crossed my mind that he might be coming around to pick up some classical records he'd loaned me, so I assumed he'd call again.

About half an hour later, the phone rang. It was John, asking whether I might be willing to join him for dinner. When I said I was tired and had no interest in resuming our relationship, he pressed on, saying he had been hoping to reach me all weekend and wanted very much to talk with me. I was genuinely reluctant because I had spent these past three weeks convincing myself that the relationship had ended and now was concentrating on moving on. But he expressed an urgent need to see me, and so, almost grudgingly, I agreed. When he came to pick me up a few minutes later, he asked whether we might eat at his house since he had already purchased things for a simple supper. When we got there, we went straight to the kitchen and he asked me to sit down at the tiny table at the back of the room. He then proceeded to take a pen in hand and began to write, first in French, then in English:

> Ma Chérie
> Enfin, je sais bien que je t'aime. Je ne peux demeurer loin de toi plus longtemps.
> Alors, je te prie, fais moi l'honneur de m'épouser. Ainsi, nous serons ensemble toute notre vie.
> Avec mes baisers ardents.

My Dear,
Finally, I know well that I love you. I cannot stay away from you any longer.
So, I beg you, do me the honor of marrying me. Thus, we will be together all our life.
With my ardent kisses.

The question having now been committed to paper, he handed it to me and then got down on his knee to ask me to marry him. With great seriousness, I examined the paper and, after a long pause, asked him what had changed. He responded without hesitation, telling me of the anguish he'd experienced during the last three weeks. He begged my forgiveness, saying that the idea of marriage and commitment had, at first, been terrifying. Thinking back to the difficulties in his own parents' marriage, their unhappiness with each other and the long separations they had maintained, had made him extremely wary of a long-term relationship with anyone. In other words, he had never seen marriage as a high priority and was ambivalent about whether he should marry at all. The separation from me, however, had given him time to reconsider his attitude and feelings. He knew, he said, that he'd been trying to deny his love for me by backing away from his initial proposal. Now, however, he was clear: he loved me and wanted me to be his wife. We cried together. I told him I loved him as well and, with great joy, would accept his proposal.

Looking back, I realize that the ambivalence expressed in the withdrawal of his initial proposal has been with us throughout most of our marriage. In one sense, John has always been a more independent person than I, demonstrating his greater need for distance and, at times, almost complete isolation. There have been periods of intense happiness, as well as months of separation and enormous sadness. In our fortieth year of marriage, I can acknowledge that we have had to work very hard to maintain our relationship. Through years of therapy, I've come to understand that the rejection I'd experienced at the hands of my mother must have led me to choose two men who were inaccessible, each in his own way. Fortunately, the physical passion that we felt for each other in the early days of our romance has remained and has helped us find our way back to each other despite many difficult times.

Three weeks after his second proposal, on December 19, 1959, we were married. It was a small wedding, with just thirty of our friends and relatives in attendance. John's mother came down from New York the night before the wedding; it was the very first time I met her. John's father couldn't attend; at the appointed time he was milking about a dozen cows. Though John's parents had never been legally separated, they lived apart after his father purchased the farm. Mary chose to remain in New York, far from the isolation and cold the farm represented, visiting only when John was there during the summer or at Christmas.

The wedding was exactly what we wanted. Since remarriage following divorce was not permitted in the Syrian Orthodox church, the ceremony was performed at a Unitarian church in Washington, followed by a dinner at one of the few French restaurants in Washington at the time, Pierre's. The walls of the room within the wonderful two-story converted mansion on Connecticut Avenue were entirely mirrored, and as it was just before Christmas, the room glittered with candelabra and poinsettias. Together, John and I planned every detail, and we were delighted with the outcome, with only one exception: the photographer, who was the father of one of my close friends, never showed up. To this day, there's never been an explanation as to why he failed to appear, and we were disappointed. But in a strange way, the lack of photographs has served to enhance our memories of the day, from beginning to end.

Two days later, we drove to the farm. Today, it seems a strange way to have spent a honeymoon, since, of course, John's mother and father were there with us. But the excitement of seeing the beautiful, snowy mountains of Pennsylvania from within a cozy farmhouse was just too appealing. We both remember those days with joy. As for Pop, John's father, from the moment I met him it was love at first sight. He was out in the barn milking the cows when I arrived, but he greeted me with his unfailing warmth and charm.

As the marriage began, there was every indication that we'd be good for each other. Despite the differences in our education and background, we were very compatible. We both loved music, good food, movies, good restaurants, baseball, long walks, and intense conversations. We were fortunate enough to live in John's aunt's house at 3056 R Street NW for the first seven months of our marriage, while she and her husband were in Africa. It's a lovely two-story house directly opposite Montrose Park in Georgetown. I remember waking on weekends to the sounds of turtledoves and tennis balls, cooing and pinging. John and I worked extraordinarily well together. His upbringing and his years of bachelorhood had prepared him for sharing the responsibilities of running a household. We cooked, cleaned, and shopped together, enjoying the laughter and sexual playfulness that went into each of those activities.

CHAPTER 11

*I*N MARCH 1960, we were thrilled to learn that I was three months pregnant. We both wanted children and saw no reason to wait. John's future at the State Department seemed secure, and while his income was not, by today's standards, large, it was adequate for us to begin to raise a family. With our housing provided rent-free, at least for the time being, I was able to leave my secretarial position at the State Department in July. There was no question in either of our minds that I would stay at home to care for our new baby. The prospect excited me, even though I realized that the adjustment might be difficult.

In late July, a little more than a month before our child was due, we received word that John's aunt, Louise Boulton, and her husband, Rud, were returning from Africa and wanted to move back into the house on R Street. It came as a shock to us, believing as we had that our housing needs were secure. But as with so many unexpected turns in our lives, what at first seemed a cause for panic quickly evolved into an opportunity when my former boss, George Dolgin, was appointed consul general in Nigeria. George and his wife, Lee, decided to sell their home on Saratoga Avenue in Bethesda, Maryland, just over the District line. We had been in the house once and loved it, a two-bedroom rambler with a beautiful garden. We managed to scrape together enough money for a down payment, borrowing from John's mother and from the Dolgins themselves. With their generous help, we were able to buy our first home.

On September 12, 1960, David Bartram Rehm was born, a golden-haired, pink-cheeked child who became the center of our existence. If I recall correctly, I spent at least three days in the hospital recuperating from the delivery, as was the custom in those days. As I think about today's rules and restrictions governing hospital stays following deliveries, I thank my lucky stars that I had the time to recover somewhat before coming home to face the prospect of caring for a newborn. When John picked us up at the hospital, we went directly to our new home, into which he had managed to move all of our belongings. After all the excitement and preparations, we were finally beginning our new life as a family.

What I didn't anticipate, and what I didn't feel prepared for, was the overwhelming feeling of responsibility attached to a job for which I had absolutely no training. All the desire to experience motherhood, plus all the preparatory reading I had done, hadn't provided me with an adequate understanding of the sense of obligation I now felt for the life of a tiny human being. Unlike many of my peers, I had done very little baby-sitting in my teens, none of it with infants. Motherhood is clearly something most of us have to learn on the job. Now, thanks to parent-training courses, both mothers and fathers can get a grasp of the basics before the moment of truth arrives.

Nor was I prepared for the loneliness that began to pervade my life. While I experienced aloneness in my early childhood, this felt different. At first, I relished it. After all, I had left a community in which I felt as though everything I did was known about or talked about. John and I were truly private people, living quietly together without the intrusion of friends and relatives. I welcomed David's waking hours—being with him and playing with him. In good weather, we took long walks around the neighborhood, or I worked in the garden as he slept in the carriage or later played in the grass. Since John drove our only car to work, I was homebound. I looked forward to the arrival of the milkman, the diaper man, the mailman, just to have someone to whom I might say hello. Of course, there were neighbors, but precious few my own age who might have understood the feelings I was having. Besides, I had no impulse to complain about my situation. I thought I could handle it by keeping up a smiling front and pushing down my feelings of sadness. I began to feel guilty about such sadness. We had a healthy, beautiful young boy, and John had a fine career. Surely I had no right to feel sad. But I did, and I knew I had to do something about it.

John's obligations at the office intensified, making it hard for him to come home until late in the evening. We did manage to have breakfast together, but frequently we were both so tired we had little to say to each other. His work, first at the Department of State and later as the first General Counsel to the Office of the Special Trade Representative, seemed to take more and more of his time and his energy. I tried to be sympathetic because I knew that his advancing career would benefit our family. At the same time, I resented the fact that he spent so little time with the baby and me. But no matter how much I complained, he remained enormously conscientious about his professional obligations, working six full days a week, from early morning until late at night.

One bright spot each weekday was a female talk-show host named Betty Groebli. Her program was broadcast around noontime, and I made a point of tuning in each day. It was a provocative and lively show, featuring guests talking with Betty about a wide range of issues, and Betty had an engaging manner and was well informed. I recall that there was listener participation, but most of all, I remember feeling comforted by Betty's on-air presence. During the period she was on the air, I could forget my loneliness and concentrate on the subject at hand. She became a long-distance friend, someone I had never met but welcomed into my home each day.

Once David's eating and sleeping patterns fell into a manageable routine, I began to think about new challenges for myself. Of course, there was plenty to keep me busy—every young mother is familiar with the variety of never-ending tasks that must be accomplished in order to keep a household with a young baby running smoothly. But I was yearning to stretch myself into areas I'd never had an opportunity to explore. Two possibilities were in my mind, and I chose to explore both: to learn to play the piano and to learn to sew.

As a young girl, I'd been enamored of the piano and took every chance I could to caress the keyboard and pretend to create fascinating sounds. Back in my days in the children's choir at Hamline Methodist Church, I would linger after each Saturday morning rehearsal, hoping that Mrs. Rawls would teach me a bit about scales and chords. She was generous with her time, but without a piano on which to practice during the week, I made little progress. Whenever I visited a friend who had a piano, I would spend time playing the few short pieces I knew, over and over again.

John supported my interest in music, so we began to watch the newspaper ads. When a Fischer baby grand piano came up for sale, we jumped. The father of a neighbor was a piano tuner and went along with us to ensure that the instrument was basically sound. I can still remember the excitement I felt watching that mahogany piano move into our living room, knowing that only my own conscience and parental obligations would keep me from immersing myself in my beloved piano music. I thought I might be able to teach myself, at least initially, since I knew the keyboard and had no ambition beyond learning to play adequately, though I realized soon enough that I needed professional guidance and a systematic approach to learning and practice. Through friends, I found an excellent teacher who played with Washington's prestigious Friday Morning Music Club and had a few adult students. Taking piano lessons involved rearranging our usual routine, and so I felt a new sense of freedom. John began leaving the car at home, at first just for the weekly piano lesson. Later, as David grew older, I took on more and more of the shopping and errands necessary to keep the household running. Venturing out for piano lessons, or even for more mundane trips to the grocery store or gas station, felt liberating after the many months at home with a newborn.

Practicing the piano was a great joy for me. To this day, I can remember my excitement when my teacher presented me with the *Handbook of Anna Magdalena Bach*. Such deceptively simple but beautiful pieces, and how I adored playing them, again and again. As I practiced, David would sit on the living room floor playing with his toys. It was there, I believe, that his own love of music began. He started piano lessons at five and ultimately majored in music and intellectual history at Oberlin. Our daughter, Jennie, who came three and a half years later, also studied piano as well as religion, at Carleton.

My other passion became sewing. Granted, this was more a solitary endeavor, but nevertheless one that gave me great satisfaction. As a young girl, I had watched my mother create dresses, coats, and suits, marveling at her ability to fashion totally professional-looking apparel that never had the whiff of "homemade" about it. Though I had taken a high school sewing course,

I knew little more than the basics, but I was confident I could learn. We bought a new Singer sewing machine, one with all the latest features. I had some inner sense that I could turn clothes-making into a money-saving venture, although I regarded it as a leap of faith on John's part since we had precious little money to spare. But he believed in me and my ability to learn, and clearly saw the ten-dollar monthly payment as an investment worth making.

With both the piano and sewing, I knew that I was expressing aspects of my childhood hunger, the wish to use my hands in creative ways. And there was something else. With sewing, I felt that I could somehow connect with my mother in a way I'd never been able to do while she was living. I could almost sense her looking over my shoulder, watching as I worked at the sewing machine, sometimes very late at night, after David had finally fallen asleep. I imagined her looking on approvingly, and even being surprised that, despite the fact that she'd given me no direct lessons, somehow I had learned from her.

I confess to being somewhat obsessive in my desire to "get it right." I followed written instructions very carefully, surprising myself when the meaning of a complicated instruction became clear to me. But the work had to be just so. If an inset sleeve didn't fit with the right amount of "ease" into the armhole, out it came, again and again. If a handmade buttonhole showed signs of fraying fabric, I went over it repeatedly until it was perfect. Such attention to detail was useful in terms of producing a finished-looking dress or blouse, but it meant many late hours at the sewing machine. This attention to detail was, in itself, a useful habit that I would later translate into other areas of work.

In addition to caring for our son and our home, playing the piano, and sewing, the other major area of interest became cooking. I loved the freedom to experiment in the kitchen, trying new recipes and occasionally inviting John's colleagues and their wives to dinner. Organization seemed to me key in approaching food preparation, especially when I was cooking for a number of people. This was another area where I know I was making up for the lack of opportunity I had had in my own home. My mother's kitchen was her own, and while my sister and I were required to set the table and do the dishes, we were never allowed to be involved in the food preparation. So, once more, I found myself experiencing an aspect of womanhood that I'd never been permitted to enjoy as a child. It was also in those early years on Saratoga Avenue that my love of gardening began to grow. I knew virtually nothing about flowers other than that I loved to look at them and smell them. Lee Dolgin had already planted a lovely garden, but it now became my responsibility to care for it, to learn how to differentiate between a weed and a seedling, to understand that different areas of the garden, depending on shade and sun, required different approaches. One morning, I became adventurous and transplanted veronica from one of the flower beds to a bare plot next to the house. I woke up the next morning at 2:00 a.m., worrying that I hadn't watered the flowers sufficiently, so out I went in my housecoat, flashlight in one hand and garden hose in the other, to ensure that the new plants would survive.

CHAPTER 12

THE ASSASSINATION OF President John F. Kennedy on November 22, 1963, was a point at which our world changed. Like most others of my generation, I remember the shock and overwhelming sorrow I felt as I heard Walter Cronkite announce his death. For days afterward, people wept openly and without shame in the street, in grocery stores, anywhere, sharing their grief with strangers. I had cast my first vote in a presidential election for Kennedy in 1960, believing that this bright, energetic, and articulate young man with his elegant wife was just the right person to lead us forward. His election marked my political awakening, the moment at which I began to be more attuned to the fascinating world of candidates, platforms, campaign speeches, and debates. Up until that point, I confess I had paid little attention to what was happening in the world, barely watching the nightly news or reading a daily newspaper.

As general counsel to the special trade representative (STR), Governor Christian Herter, John occupied an office situated in the Old Executive Office Building, since STR functioned in close coordination with the White House. On the night after the president's body was brought back to Washington to lay in state in the East Room of the White House, John and I, along with the entire STR staff, were invited to come to pay our respects. I shall never forget the solemn silence in that room that night, with the honor guard standing at attention. Though I was born and raised in Washington, this was the very first time in my life I had ever been inside the White House, and I was filled with sadness and awe.

In April 1964, Jennifer Aed Rehm was born. We were delighted to have both a boy and a girl, and felt our family was complete. By this time, David, at three and a half, was ready for preschool, and we chose a cooperative nursery school not far from our home. The advantages were twofold: a co-op was less expensive, and the experience became a new outlet for me, allowing me to meet other women who were also in the home. The group of children was small, and each parent participated with the teacher at least one morning a week.

I don't look back on those years as being terribly happy. I was not a patient person, nor was I sufficiently mature to deal with my frustration at being left virtually alone with the responsibility for two children and having very little time for myself and my own interests. I also don't think there was much acknowledgment of the kinds of feelings I was experiencing. In the early 1960s, magazines and television programs featured smiling women posing in front of their washing machines, taking great satisfaction in clean collars and soft towels. While I, too, participated in that kind of endeavor, I was restless and edgy. I can remember talking to myself in fairly stern terms, reminding myself of the fact that we had two beautiful children, a lovely home, and a secure income. But it never seemed to do the trick.

The inevitable began to happen. I started blaming John for my frustration and my lack of freedom, though I really couldn't have articulated why I was angry or even why I wanted more freedom. I only knew that on the rare occasions when he was at home, I wanted his attention. He, on the other hand, was devoting himself so entirely to his work that when he was at home, he was exhausted. He wasn't interested in hearing about my frustration and he didn't try to alleviate it. Instead of catching up on chores that had to be done around the house, he slept. I, in turn, put more and more of my frustration into creating successful dresses, blouses, and children's clothes, in which I took great pleasure and pride. I played the piano. I mowed the lawn. I did the grocery shopping. But none of that eased my unhappiness or the strain that was growing between us. John became increasingly withdrawn. We just couldn't seem to be able to find a way to be with each other. His withdrawal would prompt my outbursts; my outbursts would lead to further withdrawal. I kept thinking, If I could only find the key! I knew there was a dear, loving, warm human being inside, but I just couldn't reach him. It wasn't until many years later that I came to understand that the more I complained and criticized him, the less he cared to deal with me.

Because of John's position, we were occasionally invited out to social functions, and for those I was most grateful. It was a chance to dress up, to participate in a world where people spoke to each other, where laughter and conversation came easily. Even in those days, people would ask that awful Washington question, "What do you do?" But since most of the women I knew shared my "homemaker" status, I didn't feel the stigma to the same degree that young women today tell me they do. People complimented me on my clothes and seemed genuinely amazed when I told them I had made them myself. I also learned early on through those occasions that no matter what the subject, I could participate in the conversation by asking questions. It was something that came easily to me, and I could pose them without embarrassment. Whether the topic was a child's school experience or what the president might do in relation to the latest trade battle, I listened carefully and asked questions because I was genuinely interested in the answers. Sometimes I was even so bold as to gently challenge the answers I got. The important thing was that, despite my lack of education, I felt as though questions were an acceptable form of participation.

It was during this time that I began a course in fashion modeling, hoping to convert my interest in clothing into some aspect of the garment business. I knew I loved clothes and made them well, so I hoped the experience would help me gain confidence.

I can recall going into the studios of the Model's Guild for the first time. I felt very unsure of myself, convinced that I could never become a professional model, but the excitement of seeing other women my own age and younger rehearsing their runway walks inspired me. Some were, like me, novices, while others were old hands, willing to share tips about makeup techniques and job openings. Our efforts were critiqued by instructors, who talked with us about the length of stride, haircut or color, makeup, and, generally, how to please a fashion-show audience. Those were the days of false eyelashes (which took lots of time to apply), short haircuts for models, and little steps on the runways. The course lasted about six weeks, and at the end we put on a "show" for our spouses and friends. Though I felt more than a little foolish, I was proud that I'd learned to hold my head up and walk with a certain confidence I'd never had before. After "graduation," I did several fashion shows around the area, as well as informal modeling in local stores. One day in particular settled the question of whether I was really cut out to do the job. I was appearing in a summer luncheon fashion show at a country club in Maryland, and one of the outfits I was modeling was a bathing suit with a beach cover-up. I had been instructed to take off the robe to show the bathing suit as I walked along the runway in high heels. As the women attending the luncheon applauded, I found myself feeling ashamed, almost as though I were part of a strip show. Perhaps, without even realizing it, my mind had taken a leap back to that day at North Beach when, as a child surrounded by aunts, I had had to take off my clothes and put on my bathing suit. All of a sudden, I knew I wasn't really comfortable with this kind of work. As I left the club that day, I knew it would be the end of my modeling "career."

Though it didn't last very long, there's no question in my mind that the experience of modeling helped me feel easier about my physical self. I never appeared without racing heart or the fear that I'd fall flat on my face, but somehow, after I'd done it several times and come to realize that most of the other women around me, no matter how calm their outward appearance, felt pretty much as I did, I managed to overcome my lack of self-confidence and go out there to proudly strut the runway.

There was another element involved, and that was the pride I took in once again contributing financially to our household. There was not a great deal of money involved, but at least enough to help pay for clothing, fabrics, and makeup. It gave me a sense of independence, which began to spill over into other aspects of my life. I found myself feeling easier about making new friends, and less critical about myself in the process. I'd grown up constantly making negative comparisons between myself and those around me. Now I had some sense that I could hold my own.

Vacations during these early years were divided between North Ocean City, Maryland, and the farm. We would take a small cottage apartment at the beach for a week and, late in August, go to Pennsylvania for two weeks with Mary and Pop. The north end of Ocean City was relatively quiet at the time, and our apartment was about a hundred feet from the ocean. My only problem with driving to Ocean City was the Bay Bridge. I have a terrible fear of heights, and had to close my eyes while John drove across the span. Then, one summer, to my horror, I was forced to drive the car myself. John, David, and Jennie loved to bodysurf together, as I sat and watched from the beach. One day, I went off looking for a new bathing suit, and when I returned they were nowhere in sight. I asked the lifeguard whether he'd seen them, and he told me they'd been taken to the hospital because our son had been hurt. As I raced down the ocean high way, hideous images kept erupting in my mind. When I arrived at the hospital, however, there were David and Jennie, seated in the waiting room. I was relieved to see them both but stunned to learn that it was John who had caught a particularly rough wave and dislocated his right shoulder. He was still in the recovery room after the medics had pulled his arm back into the socket, a very painful experience. By the time our vacation was over, he was still wearing his arm in a sling attached to his body, so I had no choice but to drive, a truly unnerving experience because I had always been afraid of being pulled off the bridge. As we neared it, I asked John to start talking to me, and to keep talking for the entire crossing, so that I wouldn't look over the side and lose control of the car. I was shaking, but I managed to do it. Once was enough, though.

We spent Christmas at the farm each year, cutting down a tree and decorating the tiny house with green boughs. Although the relationship between John's parents was not particularly warm, they made an effort to be cordial and convivial when we were around. I remember most of all the delicious food that always awaited us. One Christmas, Pop ordered lobsters and clams from Damariscotta Farms in Maine. John and I drove Pop's old Jeep to the train station at Hop Bottom, Pennsylvania, to pick up a huge barrel containing the live lobsters and clams packed in ice. We brought them back and up the hill, chilled champagne bottles in the snow, and feasted for days.

During the summer of 1966, we learned that Pop was suffering from diabetic retinopathy and had lost a great deal of vision.

Up until that point, he'd relished living at the farm by himself, but with the loss of his eyesight, it was becoming increasingly difficult for him. Then, in October 1966, something terrible happened. There had been warnings of a rabid fox in the area, and on the twelfth, before dawn, Pop apparently heard a noise and took his shotgun outside to investigate. Instead of shooting a fox, however, he tripped and fell on his gun. A neighbor found him a day later, lying dead. The coroner pronounced it an accidental death. Our neighbor called us, and so the next day we drove to the farm to arrange for Pop's cremation. Much to our horror, the funeral home that had taken his body had already embalmed him by the time we arrived, a procedure that Pop in prior discussions had spoken of with loathing. But it was too late. All we could do was to ensure that the rest of Pop's wishes were carried out.

I shall never forget the look on the face of the owner of the funeral parlor when we told him that we didn't want a fancy casket, that there would be no "viewing," and that all we required was a simple wooden box. He was horrified, having assumed that we, as "city folk," would choose something very expensive and ornate, both in the way of a funeral and a casket. He kept trying to tell us that there was no such thing as a "simple wooden box," and that surely we would want to purchase a true, shiny, mahogany or walnut casket in which to transport Pop's body to the crematorium. But we held our ground, finally convincing him that we would have no such thing. In the end, we paid hundreds of dollars for a simple wooden box in which a casket had been delivered. It was an outrageous price to pay, and I realized the extent to which those in mourning are held captive by an industry that, in many cases, is totally out of tune with the feelings of the family.

We stayed at the farm for another few days, preparing to close down the house and waiting for Pop's ashes to be returned. Mary arrived, and we decided to spread the ashes around the big hickory tree in the large meadow above the house, a tree that had grown to enormous height in the twenty years that Pop had owned the land. I remember it was a beautiful day as the three of us walked up the lane that both Pop and John had walked with the cows and heifers so many times. We were quiet as we crossed the field to the hickory tree, but then, as John opened the small pine box containing Pop's ashes, we began to sing. I don't remember exactly what the song was, but our singing reminded me that early each morning, Pop would open the kitchen door and step outside in just his shirt and blue jeans, no matter what the weather, and begin la-la-la-ing. He and the sun or the clouds or the rain were always in harmony with one another, so it was fitting that we should be singing as we each took a handful and spread his ashes around the hickory tree. Even as we were engrossed in our mission, out of the corner of my eye I could see that there were people watching us. Perhaps they were hunters, or simply curious neighbors, who had come to observe these strange folks from Washington and New York as they carried out their own private funereal ritual, which, from afar, must have seemed strange indeed.

We left the farm several days later, knowing that it would never be the same again. Pop would no longer be there to greet us at Christmas or in the summertime. He would no longer be able to sit and talk and play or read with his young grandchildren, and we would no longer have the chance to laugh and talk with him. As John and I walked out the door for that last time before returning to Washington, we held each other close and promised that now we would be the ones to create our own family celebrations. He, as an only child, had known the love and respect of his father. Now we would take on the responsibility for the farm and help our children to realize how important a part of all our lives it had been, and is even now.

Meanwhile, our home on Saratoga Avenue was becoming too small for our family of four. With David and Jennie sharing one bedroom, it became increasingly apparent that we would have to begin to search for a house with additional rooms, not only for sleeping but for living. We scoured the area for a year or so, and finally, while John was out of the country, I came upon a house in which we'd attended a cocktail party the year before. It was near ours and had barely gone on the market, but there were already two other bidders so I knew I'd have to move quickly. I made a call to John in Switzerland, got his agreement, and made the bid. To our great joy, the owners accepted it and the house was ours. We had to do some fancy footwork to get all the documents signed and notarized since John wasn't expected home for another four weeks, but finally we had our new home.

The house on Worthington Drive was, and still is, perfect for us, with enough space for each of us to create a private haven. For me, that area was, and is, the sewing room, a wonderful, airy, light-filled addition to the second floor of the house, overlooking the garden. Into that room went my sewing machine, plus a small desk and chair and a daybed. The ironing board was always close by, ready for pressing a seam or ironing a shirt. Over the years, I've spent more time in that room than in any other in the house. The ironing board is gone now, as is the sewing machine. In their place is a long desk, with a computer, printer, and fax machine. But even now, after a long day at the office, I can feel myself relax as soon as I walk in there.

Our garden is fenced in, so Jennie and David could both enjoy playing on a swing and jungle gym as I worked in the sewing room. One summer day when Jennie was about seven (this was before we had installed air-conditioning, so all the windows were wide open), she called up to me as I was struggling with a particularly delicate maneuver on my sewing machine. "Mom," she said, "there's a funny-looking cat in our tree." The tree she was referring to is a large Japanese maple that sits in the center of our patio, just outside our library doors. Since I couldn't see the tree from my sewing room window, I simply said, "That's nice, Jen. Now just leave Mommy alone so I can finish what I'm doing." Less than two minutes later, she called up to me again, this time saying, "Mom, this is a really funny-looking cat, and I think you ought to see it." At this point, I was becoming irritated, so I said, more harshly than I should have, "Jen, just leave the kitty-cat alone and I'll come see it later." But fortunately Jen persisted. She said, "Well, OK, but this is a really *big* funny-looking cat." With that, she got my attention, and I went downstairs, grumbling as I went. But when I walked outdoors and looked up into the tree, I almost fainted. There was a huge ocelot perched in our maple tree! Luckily, I had the sense not to scream, because I might have frightened it and caused it to jump. I grabbed Jennie, yanked her into the house, and quickly dialed 911. Then, because we could see the creature from the safety of our kitchen window, I called Willard Scott, then a local radio personality, who happened to be on the air at that moment. I got through to someone in the newsroom, who passed the word on to Willard, who then announced on the air that there was a pretty big stray ocelot on the loose in Bethesda. Fortunately, the humane society arrived within moments, got a net over the ocelot's head, and took it away. It turned out that the creature belonged to a neighbor a block from our house, but no one in the area had known about it.

CHAPTER 13

*A*FTER THE MOVE to the new house in 1967, I found myself increasingly turning to outside activities. First came the introduction to St. Patrick's Episcopal Church in Washington. It was at the height of the civil rights movement, and ours was a dynamic parish led by a man committed to healing the racial divide in our country, the Reverend Thomas D. Bowers. Tom drew people of all backgrounds and economic status to the church, people willing to grapple with their own biases. In addition, it was a fun-loving parish, where the idea of Sunday morning worship went hand in hand with Saturday night festivities.

From the beginning of our involvement with St. Patrick's, John was less engaged than I. He had never been baptized, his parents having believed that the best they as agnostics could do for their only child was to leave him free of the "burden" of baptism. Consequently, he looked somewhat sourly on any demonstration of organized religion. He would participate in Sunday morning services "for the sake of the children," but he never seemed very happy to be there. They had been baptized shortly after birth in the Syrian Orthodox church, something I felt strongly about and which he didn't resist. He had no objections to David's and Jennie's enrollment in Sunday school, but he took little interest in their weekly classes. As Jennie grew older, however, she balked at attending either Sunday classes or church, and to my dismay, John supported her rebellion. If she wanted to stay home, he'd stay home with her.

As I came to realize, refusing to attend church was just one of the ways John was demonstrating his desire to distance himself from regular social engagements or even the intimacy of marriage. The reason given was always his workload. His concentration on work intensified even more when, after the election of Richard Nixon, he was asked to leave his post in the Office of the Special Trade Representative. John has often said that the moment when Robert Ellsworth, Nixon's senior aide, asked for his resignation was actually the high point of his career, since he'd never had any respect for Nixon and had no intention of staying on at STR under his presidency. After thirteen busy and fulfilling years in government, the idea of moving back into a private law firm both excited and terrified him. John had several offers and spent weeks considering various options. Fortunately for both of us, at a speaking engagement in New York he met David Busby, who headed up a small Manhattan firm called Busby, Rivkin, Sherman & Levy. David had recently moved from New York to Washington, with the idea of expanding the firm into the trade field, and thought John would be just the right person to join him. John's decision to go with him was the start of a wonderful thirty-year partnership and friendship for the two of them. At the same time, I am fortunate to call David's wife, Mary Beth, one of my closest friends.

The move into the world of private practice had both its

pluses and minuses. There was a widening circle of friends and social events. And there was also an increased income. But John was less than happy about the new situation, dissatisfied with his own performance and feeling the pressure of bearing the economic responsibility for a wife and two children. As he became more and more withdrawn, the atmosphere in the household became tenser and tenser. There was no hiding the tension from two very sensitive children, neither of whom knew what to do or how to react to their parents' arguments and loud accusations. John was always loving and warm toward them, when he was around. I found it more difficult to comfort them because he seemed to be using them to demonstrate that he was an affectionate and warm person but that those feelings were restricted to his children.

That is the period in my children's lives about which I feel most sad, a time when they should have been secure in the knowledge of the love and affection between their two parents. Instead, they were exposed to anger and harsh words and slammed doors, and had no idea what was happening or why. I realize that the lives of very few children are without tension, but I feel particularly guilty because there were times when, by my voice and actions, I took out my own frustrations on them, failing to recognize just how insecure they were feeling. There was one argument between John and me over money that even now makes me cringe. Sex and money, I've been told by therapists, are the two most important issues that couples have to work out, and that process can take many years. One evening, after Jennie and David had finished dinner and gone to their rooms, John and I began talking about whether we could afford to make a particular purchase for our home. The talk quickly turned to yelling. Though a concrete item was involved, it was the existing tension between us that was the source of the argument: it had risen to the surface, leading us into a shouting match. As we began to hurl accusations at each other, David, now aged eleven, came back downstairs to where we were sitting and put twenty dollars in small bills and change on the table between us. It was his total savings from his weekly allowance and his pay for extra chores he had performed. With tears in his eyes, he said, "I don't like hearing my parents arguing about money. You make me feel ashamed. So here is my money. Now maybe you'll stop." With that, he turned and left the room. John and I looked at each other, realizing that our son had demonstrated real maturity in the face of our infantile behavior.

CHAPTER 14

A S I HAD DONE in the past, I channeled my pent-up energies into outside activities, widening my circle of friends by participating in volunteer associations primarily related to the church as well as another organization called The Hospitality and Information Service (THIS). The monthly meetings of THIS brought women whose husbands were members of the foreign diplomatic community together with American wives for luncheons and other social activities. Little did I know how significant THIS would eventually prove to be in my move toward radio.

I have often thought that had the relationship between John and me been a perfect one (in truth, I've never known any couple whose relationship was perfect), perhaps I would never have looked for some way to fulfill myself outside the home. As it was, having become increasingly frustrated with his apparent lack of interest in me, his lack of willingness to communicate, and what

I perceived as a lack of joy in our lives, I decided to concentrate on finding my own satisfactions. Luckily, during those years I had female friends who, in one way or another, shared the same frustrations. We could talk on the phone and vent our anger, even laugh about the silly ways in which our marriages were flawed. The early seventies were years when young married women, with or without a college education, were just beginning to respond to Betty Friedan's *The Feminine Mystique*, asking themselves what they could do to improve their lives. With several of the women of St. Patrick's Church, I began to attend occasional evening meetings to talk about our situations and frustrations. These were early "consciousness-raising" sessions, ultimately evolving into a regular Monday night meeting at the church. The group expanded, including both men and women of varying ages, all seeking some deeper level of understanding of themselves and each other. But the core group of women, five of us in all, have become lifelong friends. One of my closest friends, Jane Dixon, began as a Sunday school teacher at St. Patrick's, then went on to seminary, was ordained as a priest, and is now the suffragan bishop of the Episcopal Diocese of Washington.

Among those women, a number had taken a course they jokingly referred to as Feminism 101, at George Washington University. In fact, its formal name was "New Horizons for Women," a course designed to assist women like me who were trying to figure out how to spend the rest of their lives. This was the fall of 1972. Our children were twelve and nine, and I knew I was becoming less and less important in their daily existence. So, with considerable trepidation, I picked up the phone one day to call GW and inquire about the one-semester course. Much to my relief, there were no educational prerequisites, and I was registered over the phone and urged to come to the first class, which was to begin in just a few weeks. I could scarcely believe I'd had the courage to do it. I think part of me expected someone on the other end of the telephone line to challenge me, to demand that I present credentials and justify my right to apply for a college course. It was even worse when I arrived at the campus on the appointed day. I felt so supremely out of place, ready to be told that whoever I'd talked with on the telephone had made a mistake in encouraging me to come. I'm uncomfortable even now recalling just how intimidated I felt. First of all, I had never before been on any kind of college campus, except to attend a football game at the University of Maryland. Second, I believed that somehow everybody could tell that I had no college degree to my credit (something like an invisible stamp of NO DIPLOMA on my forehead).

After an introduction by the director of the program to the entire group of some 150 women, we were divided up according to the amount of education we'd had. In other words, the Ph.D.'s went to a classroom on the top floor, those with a master's went to another spot, those who'd completed their undergraduate degree went to the next floor, and those of us who'd never been to college shared a classroom on the first floor. This was unfortunate. Those of us in the "no college ed" classroom joked uncomfortably, knowing that we had somehow been set apart and perhaps even stigmatized by our placement even before we began doing anything. Ours was the smallest group and perhaps the oldest, reflecting the lesser stress on higher education that had been prevalent at the time I graduated from high school. It was indeed segregation by education. I understand that GWU has since changed the entire approach of the course, including blending together those of different educational backgrounds.

Once we got over the initial shyness about our placement, we were urged to share something about our backgrounds with the rest of the class, plus any thoughts about what we aspired to or how we saw the future unfolding. At the time, having become a fairly proficient seamstress, I had it in mind that perhaps fashion design might be a field to pursue. Alternatively, I thought about beginning to take college courses, perhaps with the idea of eventually seeking a degree, the lack of which had begun to nag at me. But much to my surprise, those within our group began to urge me to try broadcasting.

To this day, I'm not clear why. I know I entered into the group discussion fully, not only offering details of my own background but also commenting and asking questions about other women's stories. These women were all interesting, most of them married with children, reaching out, as I was, for some unknown future beyond the obligations of wife and mother. But I was totally taken aback by the degree to which they encouraged me to venture into a field for which I had absolutely no background or preparation. I can only speculate that because of my ability to speak out within the small group in ways most of them felt unprepared to do, they saw me as someone who could succeed in some aspect of broadcasting, where the number of women (at that time) was very small. I can't tell you now, more than twenty-five years later, exactly what affected me so strongly during that semester. Perhaps it was the opportunity to share my stories and hear those of others in a setting that seemed to invest the exchanges with a sense of importance, to lend a certain sense of reality and solidity to our experiences. Whatever it was, I felt a new optimism, as though, somehow, something would happen. And, miraculously, it did.

At the time, I was continuing my volunteer work for The Hospitality and Information Service. Through that work, I met the wife of a Canadian diplomat, Fay Armstrong, whose husband worked on trade matters and had come to know my husband professionally. We saw each other fairly regularly, and on one occasion, shortly after I'd completed the "New Horizons" course, Fay mentioned to me that she'd begun working as a volunteer at WAMU-FM on a new program called "The Home Show." Back then, wives of foreign diplomats were not permitted to hold paying jobs in this country, so she was delighted to have found something she could do that was challenging and intellectually satisfying. As she talked about her work helping to put together daily programs for on-air discussions, finding guests, and researching material, something happened to me. If I were to draw you a cartoon depiction of that moment, you would see a lightbulb going on above my head. It was a crucial moment in my life because I saw it as a clear signal that this idea of doing something in broadcasting might be a real possibility.

"Do you suppose they could use any additional volunteers?" I asked. She smiled warmly and said she would be glad to ask the producer and host of the program, Irma Aandahl, if there might be room for one more. I remember feeling as though this was something that could turn into one of the luckiest moments of my life, and yet being afraid to imagine it. Within a day or two, Fay telephoned to ask whether I was still interested. Was I interested? Of course! Fay gave me Irma's number and said she was expecting my call and could see me sometime the following week. The next Monday, I went to WAMU's studios on the campus of American University, which, as it turned out, was no more than three minutes from my home. Nevertheless, in my nervousness about finding my way and being on time, I had John drive me past the studio (it looked like a huge Quonset hut) the day before the meeting. This was a habit I realized I had gotten into—being leery of new places, fearing I'd get lost. It's a feeling that's with me even now.

Walking into the studio that day to meet Irma was so exciting, and yet I was afraid she would find some reason to turn me down. After all, I told myself, here I was on a college campus with no college education of my own. Did I really think I had something of substance to offer Irma and her staff? My doubts were raging inside, focusing on all sorts of weaknesses I perceived in myself, but from the minute I met Irma and her producer, Margaret West, I felt comfortable.

Irma and Margaret were cordial and welcoming, giving me a general idea of the planning and coordination involved in putting together a daily three-hour broadcast. Ninety minutes of that three hours was the portion on which we would work together, along with Fay Armstrong. We would all be expected to come up with program ideas, find guests, and research every subject. It was agreed that I would come in to start my volunteer activity the following Monday. I couldn't believe my good fortune. Here was an opportunity to learn about the broadcast medium I'd revered for so long, and, at the same time, delve into subjects that were of interest to me. Throughout that week, I was like a child waiting for Christmas to come.

Part Two

A VOICE OF MY OWN

CHAPTER 15

*W*HEN THE DAY finally came, the children went off to school and I prepared myself for my first morning at WAMU-FM. I had to make a great effort to quiet my negative inner voices, and I did so by looking in the mirror and speaking out loud to myself, saying over and over again that I must put my fears aside so that no one would know how afraid I was. I tried to imagine walking into the building, introducing myself, smiling, and appearing calm and self-assured. It was an exercise in attempting to use my imagination to modify my behavior.

I got to the studio earlier than my scheduled 8:00 a.m. arrival time and was met at the door by a tall, slender woman who introduced herself as station manager Susan Harmon. She asked whether I was the new volunteer and then told me that, unfortunately, Irma Aandahl was going to be out sick. My heart sank, thinking that my introduction to the workings of radio was not to be, but Susan went on to say that she would be sitting in for Irma, hosting the show, and that she would like me to join her in the studio. I couldn't believe my ears, but said I'd be happy to do whatever I could to help out.

It's important to understand that way back in 1973, public radio was just beginning to get off the ground. National Public Radio was a little-known broadcast entity, and WAMU was a small member station with just two or three full-time staff members. It was a time of growth and experimentation, a time when an inexperienced person like me could venture onto the airwaves without training, as long as she had something to say. The miraculous part was how natural it all felt, walking into the broadcast studio for the first time, gazing at the four microphones on the large round table, looking through the glass as the engineer readied the tapes and adjusted the voice levels.

The guest that day was a woman from the Dairy Council, touting the importance of milk, butter, and eggs in the daily diet. Given today's high concentration on matters of politics, hazardous foods, and sex on the Internet, the topic was quite tame, and I felt comfortable with it since I knew something about the subject. After all, as the mother of two young children, I'd worried about providing my family with wholesome, nourishing foods, and I'd read a lot. Indeed, I'd read enough to know that concern was already growing about the recommended amount of dairy products in our overall food intake, as well as about the effects of eggs and fatty meats on longevity. In addition, our son, David, had developed an allergy in infancy to both cow's and goat's milk, so finding a suitable substitute had entailed learning as much as I could about other possible products.

Following Susan Harmon's lead, in a polite but firm way I put questions to the young woman, challenging her sweeping statements that dairy products and meats were absolutely essential to a healthy diet. She talked a great deal about the importance of having foods from each of the groups represented in our daily diets, while I continued to wonder out loud about the structure of the "food pyramid" that was so accepted at the time. We took several calls from listeners, who seemed genuinely interested and were looking for more information. At the end of the ninety-minute program (an awfully long time to talk about the food groups, I must admit), I was exhilarated. I felt as though I had crossed into another world, one in which words had magically expanded and held an importance that I'd never quite grasped before. What was most remarkable to me was that I had virtually no jitters, no thought of people out there listening to those of us in the studio; all that mattered was the personal conversation going on among us. In other words, it felt natural. I've wondered over the years whether that lack of stage fright came from my years of pleasure listening to the radio, or whether it came from years of acting in school and community plays, when I forgot everything other than what I knew I had to do. Whatever the source, I felt grateful that my first time on the air had been so rewarding and hadn't been a disaster. Probably if I'd known beforehand that I was going to be asked to participate in the program, I would have been a nervous wreck. Maybe sometimes it's best just to dive in.

At the age of thirty-seven, without even realizing what had happened, I had embarked on my career in radio. To reinforce my feelings of satisfaction, Susan was complimentary—she was pleased with my ease and directness and felt I'd raised issues she was sure were of interest to listeners. Yet even though I very much wanted to believe her and felt good about the broadcast, there was a part of me that wondered whether she felt obliged to say a kind word to a total novice. In any case, from that day on I was hooked. Those ninety minutes on the air, one of the most exciting times of my life, were the beginning of my adult love affair with radio.

It's now been more than twenty-five years since that day, and during that time I've had an extraordinary opportunity to do something I'm very proud of. But as with anything worthwhile, the years haven't been without difficulties, both professional and personal. I know my journey hasn't been unique; clearly women in a variety of professions have been forced to make adjustments in their lives that they never imagined in pursuing a professional dream. Of course, I may use the word "professional" today, but back then I really didn't think in those terms. My idea as I began was that this was an adventure: I would be delving into an area I didn't know and had no training for, a volunteer job I would do to the best of my ability. I had no long-term dream or plan that somehow this would turn into a real "career." To my mind, only women who were trained as doctors or lawyers (and there were precious few of them in 1973) merited "career" status; I was just determined to do the best I could to measure up, to offer good, workable ideas for consideration, and to find the best people I could to talk about them. Curiously, it was John who, almost from my earliest days on the job as a volunteer, said something to the effect that "eventually you'll have your own program." At the time, I attributed that kind of thinking to his general optimism, especially when it came to our children. Whenever they had doubts about homework or an assignment, it was John who encouraged them and helped them to believe they could achieve. Despite the periods of severe strain between us, it was clear that he believed in my ability to overcome, by sheer force of energy, diligence, and effort, whatever shortcomings I perceived in myself.

The early days at WAMU, so filled with nervous excitement, also created a certain amount of chaos in our home. First of all, each morning, instead of sitting down to a leisurely breakfast with time for us to talk as a family, I was leaving the table quickly to get myself and everyone else out the door. It seems like a small thing, but it disrupted a pattern of many years. I also used the time at breakfast to listen to John's, or Jennie's and David's, program ideas. Part of me joyously anticipated each new day at the station, while deep down I felt a certain selfishness, as though I had no right to upset the pattern to which we'd all become accustomed. But I knew I had to be "selfish" if I wanted to do something other than be at home. I do think there was a genuine pleasure on the children's part that I was doing something interesting and stimulating, though they would never have said so outright. It wasn't until some years later, when they had both finished college, that they told me how proud they'd been of what I'd accomplished.

Once the kids were out the door, I could turn my full attention to going through the newspaper, looking for story ideas or finding information to update programs airing that week. After all the years of focusing my attention on the house, car pools, cooking, and sewing, the prospect of driving the car to an office on the campus of a nearby university delighted me. For ten months, I worked every day as a volunteer, putting in as many hours as were needed but always making an effort to be home by the time the children returned from school. If there were piano lessons or doctors' appointments or school-related activities, I managed to be there. Grocery shopping had to be squeezed in, and there was dinner to make, which normally didn't get on the table until about seven-thirty. That was somewhat late for David and Jennie, but it did mean that on many nights, we could all have dinner together. As with many families, though, dinners weren't always pleasant and happy affairs; sometimes there was nothing but silence between John and me, while each of us tried to make small talk with the children.

David and Jennie learned to cook at an early age. They were both in the kitchen with me, taking partial responsibility for the preparation of meals. On the evenings when John and I went out, David would cook for the two of them. Frozen foods were not part of our regime; I shopped two or three times a week for fresh meats, chicken, fish, and vegetables. I suppose I could have made life a lot easier on myself by purchasing prepared foods, but my sense of pride wouldn't allow me to do that. After all, I said to myself, I could manage to do everything I had to do.

To use the word "balancing" doesn't really address the different directions in which I felt I was being pulled. My obligations at home were ever-present. At the office, subjects such as "Plate Tectonics" or "Global Warming" or "Sudden Infant Death Syndrome" or "Open Adoption" or "U.S.-Soviet Relations" or "The Comet Kohoutek" were occupying my mind. I was learning each day not only about the subjects at hand but also about the people in this city who were knowledgeable about such subjects. Irma and "her girls," as we were known, spent a great deal of time making telephone calls, looking for the most informed, articulate people to come to the studio as guests on the program. In the beginning, we had a lot of explaining to do about what the program actually was and what we were trying to accomplish. Most people had never heard of National Public Radio, much less "The Home Show," so we had to do something of a selling job. But little by little, the word got around that the program was worthwhile, that it provided a forum for solid discussion of a variety of topics. Every day, the person who'd taken charge of researching the subject and finding the guests would sit at the table with Irma for the on-air discussion. She was an excellent moderator, ensuring that all parties were engaged, bringing in as much background material as possible. Regularly, there were three or four people in the studio at any given time, all of whom participated in the conversation. Irma, Margaret, Fay, and I got along extremely well, primarily because Irma created an atmosphere of cooperation, with a focus on clear presentation and an understanding of each issue. Of course, there was always a certain amount of healthy competitiveness among us to bring in ideas that would be deemed sufficiently interesting for a program.

I began doing occasional restaurant reviews during that period, and that was great fun. John and I loved trying out new restaurants, so I would carry my little notebook with me, jot down a few ideas, and, several days later, make comments on the air about each new place. It was a way to combine my love of good food and good restaurants with the radio program. I was also particularly interested in medical topics. It was a time when attitudes about the medical profession and the doctor-patient relationship were beginning to shift, away from the doctor as all-knowing decision maker and toward a greater partnership between the doctor and the patient.

A number of my women friends were critical of my decision to offer my services to the radio station as a volunteer. At a time when women were striving to be recognized for their contributions to society, they felt I shouldn't be "giving away" my time and effort. I was stung by their comments, but I had a very different perspective. I saw what I was doing as an apprenticeship, learning on the job from a respected professional who was willing to share her knowledge with me. The fact that I wasn't being paid seemed of lesser importance; it was like going to a training school without paying tuition. Of course, I have to acknowledge that had my family's financial circumstances been different, I wouldn't have had the luxury or the freedom to work without pay.

After I'd been in the volunteer position for ten months, our producer, Margaret West, announced that she was leaving to give birth to her first child. Margaret had been born in Wales and trained as an attorney; she then decided that the practice of law here in the U.S. was not something she aspired to, and turned her talents to broadcasting. With her delightful accent, she always lent spirit and intelligence to our discussions. Her departure set off all kinds of anxieties in me. Should I apply to replace her? Though her paid position was part-time, I realized that the transition from volunteer status to paid status would carry with it a psychological obligation that I hadn't previously felt. Also, I was afraid to apply, an anxiety born of a fear of disappointment. Part of me thought it would be better to remain as a volunteer because it carried less risk. And yet that inner drive pushed me to consider applying for her position. John and I talked it over at length, and he urged me to make the application. This was one of the contradictory elements in our relationship. No matter how estranged we might be, when a work-related issue needed exploring, we would turn off our feelings of anger toward each other and succeed in discussing the pros and cons like a true husband and wife. I was dealing with my feelings of educational inferiority again, and he was encouraging me to put them aside and move forward.

Since American University was an institution of higher education, I worried that the authorities there would be disinclined to hire someone with only a high school background. On the other hand, I knew the work, and Irma seemed to be pleased with my performance. So, after several days of mulling it over, I took the plunge and told her I was interested in the job. She seemed to take my interest quite seriously, which was a good sign, and said she'd let me know when she'd made her decision. Days later, when I'd almost given up hope, Irma told me that she would like me to be her assistant producer. I was overjoyed.

Each day brought new ideas. As I read newspapers, watched television, or talked with friends about what was happening in the world, my head filled with possible show topics. There was so much I wanted to know, and selecting a subject meant that I would have a chance to read and organize material for its presentation on the program. Virtually nothing was off limits. I can remember organizing programs on aspects of medicine, economics, nutrition, science, the arts, cooking, sewing, education, and nursing-home care. In those early days of the program, we placed little emphasis on purely political topics, since our primary audience consisted of women in their homes and it was assumed that they just wouldn't be interested! Yet we never seemed to lack for topics, since those of us who worked on the program were all avid consumers of information. We had to be persistent and persuasive, selling the program to each potential guest.

In time, more volunteers came in to work with us. Occasionally, when Irma was out sick or took a day off, I would be the substitute host. It was a heady experience, but at times nerve-racking. Since the audience was quite small, getting people to call in wasn't always easy; especially in those early days, before talk radio had become the ubiquitous phenomenon it is today, listeners were content to sit back and participate passively in the conversation rather than dash to a phone and chime in with their own opinions or questions. I can remember sweating through many a morning, either with Irma or on my own, when, no matter how many times we offered our studio phone number, virtually no one called. It made me realize that, whatever the subject or however few calls we received, I would have to be prepared to help keep the conversation going until the hour was up. I had to force my brain to keep delving, looking for some nuance in a guest's response that would lead to a follow-up question. It was excellent training for the kind of attentive listening that is a necessity in this line of work. In fact, it was an ideal job. I saw every day as an opportunity to expand my understanding of the world around me by finding a single topic about which I wanted to know more and pursuing it. I was working with women I admired and respected, and I was learning more and more about radio. Irma was generous with her encouragement, and willing to teach me techniques of recording and editing. I watched as she took razor blade to tape, listened as she manipulated the reels of tape until the sound of a word at a crucial point became clear. I watched as she made the careful diagonal slice, eliminating the unwanted or unnecessary bit of sound, and then joined the two diagonals together with editing tape. It seemed like magic, but making that perfect splice without a blip in the sound took practice. Today, that kind of tape editing has largely been eliminated, thanks to digital equipment.

CHAPTER 16

SOMETHING HAPPENED during this early period of work that I know was important to my thinking about myself. Up until 1974, I had never had a checking account of my own; though we had a joint account, John paid all the bills from a large desktop checkbook. He handled every aspect of our financial life, from the mortgage to the utilities and charge-account bills. One afternoon early in December, I went Christmas shopping, looking for a specific pair of pajamas that John wanted. I must have gone to three or four different stores before finally finding the exact pair he'd asked for. To my annoyance, I discovered that this particular store wasn't covered by my Washington shopping plate (this was in the days before we all became accustomed to shopping with Visa, MasterCard, and American Express). I didn't have enough cash to cover the purchase, so I was forced to drive all the way home to pick up a check from my husband's checkbook and then head back to the store.

By the time I got back home an hour later, I was fuming, determined to tell John that I must have a separate account, with a small purse-sized checkbook I could carry with me all the time. But when I broached the subject that evening, John balked, finding one reason after another why this would not be a good idea. He said it would be confusing, that it would interfere with his system of "keeping track" of our finances, and that I could just as easily take a check with me whenever I needed to. I argued that I never knew when I might need one. Besides, I said, I was now earning an income, however small, and wanted to have more of a say in our financial affairs. I was very proud of the fact that I was contributing to the household income, and felt that my opinions on how we spent our money should carry greater weight. He was clearly angry. But I refused to back down and went the very next day to the bank to open an account, knowing full well that there would be retribution of some sort. For the next three weeks, John barely spoke a word to me. No matter how I tried, it was clear that my expression of independence was threatening to him in ways I couldn't fully appreciate at the time. Using silence as a weapon was something he'd begun to do habitually, knowing how the withdrawal of ordinary conversation raised my anxiety levels to intolerable heights. We fell into a pattern: withdrawal of communication on his part, followed by emotional outbursts on my part, followed by even more intense withdrawal on his part.

The checkbook incident crystallized for me my yearning for greater independence. Up until that point, I was sufficiently content with my situation that I chose not to rock the boat. But that purse-sized checkbook came to symbolize larger aspects of our marriage, namely, John's need for control over me and my tendency to allow him to exert that control. At the time, I couldn't have put it so concisely; I simply knew that our relationship was strained, and becoming increasingly difficult. As I talked with my close friend Jane Dixon about my frustration, she urged me to see a therapist. My initial response was that I could work things out if only John would change his ways. At that point, I had no conception of how my own behavior might be contributing to this tormenting psychological dance the two of us were engaged in. But as the tension mounted, affecting not only the two of us but our children as well, I decided to embark on the road to therapy.

Like many other people, I believed at the time that a few sessions with a therapist would provide quick and easy answers to the problems in our marriage. I was looking for what I imagined were techniques that other couples used to get beyond the rough places, ways of working out our differences that would leave both of our egos intact. But John made it clear from the outset that he had no interest in seeing a therapist; he simply tuned out when I mentioned the name of a female psychotherapist who'd been recommended to me. I knew that trying to persuade him to join me would be useless, but I was determined to see someone, and so, with shaky voice and sweating palms, I made the appointment.

The first few sessions with Dr. Margaret Garrett convinced me that the road to emotional health and a happy marriage was going to be a long and arduous one. Rather than allowing me to concentrate on how I felt about the marriage, she forced me to begin to examine my feelings, thoughts, and behavior patterns, not only with regard to John but also with regard to my children and friends. It was the beginning of a long process to try to understand how my tone of voice and the words I chose could have a negative effect on the people about whom I cared the most. I was, of course, very deeply set in the habit of blaming all my unhappiness on others, in feeling sorry for myself and constantly looking for hurts to justify my feelings of low self-worth. Because that's what it came down to: I just didn't feel very good about myself. Even in my work at the station, for all the joy it gave me, I couldn't overcome the constant self-criticism I heaped on myself. It was as though there was a voice inside telling me that no matter what I did or how others might praise me, there was no truth to what they were saying. I kept hearing my mother warning me to shut up, or seeing her make a threatening gesture, as though she were ready to strike me. However, my growing realization of what I was doing to myself didn't stop me from continuing what had become habitual behavior. Rather than contain the self-criticism, I would look for a way to unburden myself, and John became a convenient scapegoat. By that I don't mean to exonerate him from his part in the difficulties we were experiencing—he clearly had his own problems. But my blaming him for all the sadness and inadequacy I was feeling not only was unjust but was driving the two of us farther and farther apart.

After a few sessions, the psychotherapist recommended that I enter one of her mixed groups, made up primarily of women but with a few men, too. She shared leadership of the group with a cotherapist, an African-American male. At first, I couldn't imagine opening myself to this group of strangers, especially with men in the group. We were all, of course, pledged to confidentiality, but in the beginning I was not trustful. Little by little, however, as I listened to others in the group, I found myself drawn into participating more fully, sharing my disappointments, anxiety, and anger.

As I try to explain what happened during those two years in which I took part in that group, I realize how very inadequate ordinary language is in translating the process of therapy. The experience of participation and sharing seemed to have a freeing effect, the beginning of a process of lifting or lightening a burden. Sometimes that lightness might last a few hours; at other times, a few days. On certain occasions, I would leave a therapy session feeling even worse than I had when it began. Each of us had stories to tell, mostly related to our family histories or relationships. At the time, of course, I thought that my own experience was unique, that everyone else around me had parents who adored them and supported them in their endeavors. What I learned during those and subsequent years of therapy is that many people feel exactly as I do. They believe their parents have let them down and spend a lifetime stuck in that position, continuing to blame their parents for all the hurts they suffer.

Sometimes therapy seemed rewarding, as though I could actually feel myself making progress. A slight smile or word of support from either therapist would reassure me that I was moving in the right direction. At other times, I was certain that I was wasting my time and money. All of us, both men and women, wanted to be the favorite patient. Any gesture or word from either of the leaders would be jealously watched or listened to. All of us secretly yearned to be thought of as insightful and comprehending, as the "star pupil." Talking since then to others who've participated in group therapy, I realize that these feelings are a part of the process leading toward understanding of self, perhaps giving patients (or "clients") a restructured "family environment" in which to relive their childhood anxieties and competition for parental attention.

Attendance was mandatory, unless we were sick. That meant that few excuses went down very smoothly as far as the group was concerned. Once during that period, I accompanied John on a business trip to Cuba. Our transportation had been arranged for us, and the trip back to Miami was by chartered plane. When we got to the airport at the appointed time, we were told we'd been bumped off the charter by Congressman Ron Dellums and his staff. Protesting was fruitless. After waiting five hours while our escort attempted to make alternate arrangements, he took us back to a hotel on the beach for the night. Much to our distress, we had no access to a telephone and couldn't call home to tell our children about the delay. They were, of course, extremely worried, but there was no way to get a message to them, so we used our time to take a swim in the beautiful blue waters of the Caribbean. When we finally caught a tiny commuter plane out

My parents' wedding,
April 1929

Uncle George,
Aunt Julia, Aunt Victoria,
Daddy, Aunt Wadia,
Aunt Fahima, and
Uncle Toufic in the back
row, with Grandfather
and Grandmother seated

Mama,
1930

Mama holding me —
aged eighteen months

Standing in front of
Georgette with Sam
on the right, 1941

Roller-skating.
I'm on the left, age 14.

With Bill Roberts at the
senior prom, June 1954

Photograph that
appeared in the
Washington Post, 1954

My wedding to
George Hamaty,
October 16, 1955.
Georgette is fourth
from left, Mama
seated third from
right, Dad second
from right.

Baby
John Rehm,
age 2, with
his father

John on the
farm

My modeling
career, 1965

With the children, 1968

With Jennie, 1973

The family, Easter, 1975

For TV interview, 1982

With David in Paris, 1984

With Georgette, 1984

The family, 1984, at our twenty-fifth wedding anniversary celebration

With John in Venice, 1984

The station's softball team. I'm seated second from right, Jennie on my left.

Oliphant's cartoon for the tenth anniversary of my show, 1989

With President
Carter . . .

Salman Rushdie . . .

Newt Gingrich . . .

and Art Buchwald

Receiving an honorary degree, Western Maryland College, 1992

With Hillary Rodham Clinton and engineer Toby Schreiner

Surrounded by my producers (left to right): Nancy Robertson,
Anne Adams, Elizabeth Terry, and Sandra Pinkard, 1998

At the Thirty-fifth Multiple Sclerosis Fashion Show Luncheon, May 4, 1999

the next day, we had to fly through treacherous, stormy weather into Miami, one of the most hair-raising experiences I've ever had. When I went to group the following week, much to my shock the members and the therapists were furious with me, refusing to take my story about the appropriated charter flight as a valid excuse for missing the session. One young woman was particularly angry because I hadn't been present when she'd spoken of a terrible experience she'd had as a child. I can recall how frustrated I felt when even my explaining that telephones hadn't been available to call home did not placate them. It was a lesson to me about just how emotionally invested each of us was in group participation. At the end of two years, I felt I'd gained a great deal of insight into my relationship with my parents, and had come to realize how my interactions with others might be interpreted in ways I didn't intend. That two years, however, rather than marking the end of therapy, turned out to be only the beginning of many more years of intense self-examination.

Despite my ongoing feelings of inferiority, I forced myself to push ahead with programming ideas. After I had been at the station for about a year as a paid employee, I approached Irma with the idea of putting together a weekly half-hour program on some of the new aspects of medicine that were beginning to attract public attention. I was particularly interested in research showing a relationship between the mind and the body—for so long, physicians had considered the health of the body as distinct from the health of the mind. But now there was growing excitement about the impact on physical health of techniques such as meditation, directed imagery, and biofeedback. I wanted to explore some of these new ideas with doctors and researchers from all over the country.

Irma went to bat for me with the station's program director, Bill Brown. Together, they decided that I should have the opportunity to present a thirteen-week series, which they would then evaluate. With great excitement, I began lining up professionals to talk about the effects of meditation on headaches, the various uses of acupuncture, biofeedback and its effectiveness in lowering blood pressure, the importance of dreams, and many other subjects. At about the time I was looking for a title for the show, T. George Harris, a friend of the Busbys', came to town. T. George had been the founding genius of the very successful magazine *Psychology Today*. When I told him of my idea for the program, he was delighted, since his magazine examined many of the same issues. It was T. George who came up with the title of "Mind and Body." It was simple, direct, and perfect.

In addition to my work as associate producer of "Kaleidoscope" (the new name of "The Home Show"), I took on total responsibility for "Mind and Body." That meant choosing topics, lining up guests, arranging for studio taping time, finding background material, doing research, and preparing scripts. It was a heady experience, knowing that I was creating something new in a field that until then hadn't been explored in any series of broadcasts. Virtually all the specialists I talked with were also excited about the chance to present their ideas on a radio program. I would see a name mentioned, or hear about work that a health professional was involved in, and I'd follow up with a telephone call. Rarely did people turn me down; they were as pleased as I was.

At the end of the thirteen weeks, Irma told me that the show was just fine and that I should go on doing exactly what I was doing. She was always encouraging and supportive. Even when I felt that a particular segment hadn't measured up to my own expectations, she'd find a way to point out the positive elements contained in the discussion. After "Mind and Body" had been on the air for several months, a representative of George Washington University Medical Center approached me to ask whether I'd be interested in hosting a weekly, hour-long call-in medical program using doctors from GW. The plan was to bring a lot of medical specialists on the air to focus on a wide range of ordinary health issues, from childhood vaccinations to menopause, from sports injuries to nearsightedness. I was certainly interested in the idea, but since it was to be broadcast on WAMU, I wondered whether Irma would want me to have another hour of airtime. When I told her about the proposal, she was delighted: she thought that a weekly call-in show focusing exclusively on health topics would be a real service to listeners. I made it clear at the outset that it would have to be GW's responsibility to find the guests for the topics we chose, since I had quite enough on my plate at the moment. The partnership ultimately worked well, and the program, which we named "Health Call," won a few awards.

By this time, in the spring of 1976, I'd worked for WAMU for three years: ten months as a volunteer, and a little more than two years as a paid part-time employee. Several friends asked whether I'd given any thought to moving to television. At the time, there were no medical spots on local television news programs here in Washington, and it was conceivable that there could be a place for one of my "Mind and Body" segments. I had a long list of topics and guests I'd pursued, and thought that some of these could be translated to television. Once again, though I had little confidence that I could interest a television station in taking on an unknown, nearly forty-year-old woman with no television background, I forged ahead. Meeting with the news director of the local CBS affiliate, Jim Snyder, at what was then WTOP-TV, I showed him my list of topics and guests and explained why I thought medical subjects would be of interest to his television audience. He listened intently, asked a few questions, and looked over the list. When I finally paused, Jim, much to my surprise, said he liked the idea and urged me to come back that very afternoon to talk with a producer. Typically, I'd been totally prepared for rejection on the spot. I expressed amazement and appreciation that he would move so quickly on a matter I'd assumed would take a lot of deliberation, and reminded him that

I knew absolutely nothing about television, but he assured me I didn't have to worry on that score: others would help me learn what I needed to know in order to translate my ideas to the small screen.

After lunch with two friends, I went back to WTOP to go over various ideas with the producer, and we agreed that we would begin with a segment on biofeedback. The neurologist I had previously interviewed for "Mind and Body" was quite willing to allow the television cameras into his laboratory to tape a segment. I would be the subject of the demonstration, hooked up by a nurse to a device that would indicate my vital signs, including heartbeat, pulse rate, and blood pressure. The aim of biofeedback is to help the patient begin to control, and ultimately lower, blood pressure and pulse rate with a view toward, for example, lessening the discomfort of a headache. We worked for hours on that piece in what for me was a firsthand demonstration of the enormous differences between live radio and television. With radio, you prepare your materials, bring in the guests, and open the microphones. For television, the process is so much more complicated, with each shot requiring several "takes" from different angles and checks and rechecks for lighting, distance, tone, color, and ambient noise. What would ultimately become a three-minute piece took at least eight person-hours to prepare. There was not only the actual taping but the follow-up: working with an editor, doing voice-overs, writing introductory material. The total preparation time took several days. During that period, I was running back and forth between WAMU and WTOP to ensure that all my obligations were met. Finally, my very first medical segment went on the air during the evening news broadcast. Friends and family members called to congratulate me, underscoring for me the pervasiveness of television as compared to radio. Several people actually wrote letters commending the piece. But I was not satisfied. Even from my amateur vantage point, I realized I had a great deal to learn about this medium, and I wasn't quite sure where the learning was going to come from. By all indications, the producer felt it was his responsibility simply to get the piece on the air. The cameraman and the soundman both tried to be helpful, but I had no real sense as to how what I was doing could be done more effectively.

A day after the piece ran, I spoke with Jim Snyder and asked him whether he liked it and whether I'd have an opportunity to do a second one. He was mildly encouraging. When I told him I was about to go on a week's vacation, he suggested I put work aside and simply enjoy the time away, assuring me that when I returned we would talk about a second piece. With that assurance, I decided it was time to resign my position at WAMU. After all, I reasoned, I hadn't been able to give my full time and attention to radio, focusing instead on the television project. It wasn't fair to Irma and the others working on "Kaleidoscope," whose workload had been made heavier by my periodic absences. Besides, I thought, it was time for a new challenge, and I was ready for it. Irma had anticipated my action and, as usual, was encouraging. She had seen the piece on WTOP-TV and made some instructive comments, including a reminder not to blink so often. She said she had long thought I was a "natural" for television, and wasn't surprised at my decision to pursue that course. Susan Harmon, WAMU's manager, was equally supportive and wished me well. It was agreed that for as long as possible, I would continue with my independent production of the two health programs for radio on a volunteer basis.

When John and I returned home from Caneel Bay, I called Jim for an appointment and talked with him about a number of possible ideas. We settled on breast cancer, hoping to stress the importance of self-examinations and regular mammograms, and he told me that I would be working with the same producer. And then the problems began. The producer was working on other projects and kept postponing our initial meeting. When we finally sat down together, his ideas about the project seemed very different from mine, but since he was the seasoned professional, I acquiesced. After we'd worked on the piece for a day or two, however, I was informed that, rather than taping footage of live people, we would use slides. I was horrified, and told him I disagreed with his judgment. He was firm in his decision, however, and after several days' work, the piece went on the air. It was long, perhaps four minutes. It was slow. It dragged. It was awful. I was at the studio when it was broadcast, and after it was over Jim Snyder called me into his office. I can still recall the distress I felt, because I knew what was coming. And I can still hear his words. He said, "Diane, when you came into this office several weeks ago, I thought you were the one in a million who could do television without any training at all. I thought you were a natural. You're not. You're good, but you're not good enough. You'll have to get your training elsewhere. If you want to pursue television, I would urge you to go off to a small station, like Buffalo, get your on-air experience, learn the business for two or three years, and then come back. If you do that, I'm sure we'll find a place for you when you return."

Though a part of me had expected the bad news, I was stunned, almost to the point of tears. I forced myself to be calm. I told him I wanted to learn from the experience and asked him how much of the problem with the piece could be traced to what I myself had done, and how much of the problem could be attributed to the way it was done. He looked at me very intently and said, "I know what you're getting at, Diane, but it's still no go." I interpreted that to mean that he understood that some of the judgments had been out of my hands but that nevertheless his decision stood. I was out. Much as I appreciated his suggestion that I go to Buffalo for several years, that was out of the question. I knew that my home was here in Washington, that my primary responsibility was to my family, and that there would be no possibility of going elsewhere to learn the business.

That day stands out vividly in my memory. Even now, it's

painful to think about. Having relinquished my position at WAMU, and now having failed in my effort to move to WTOP-TV, I felt utterly bereft, as though my short-lived career in broadcasting had come to a complete dead end. I have rarely felt so dejected. I had been given the chance of a lifetime, I thought, and I had failed.

As I write these words and recall that very painful day, I am sitting at my desk on the fourth floor of the WAMU offices on Brandywine Street. Looking out my window, directly across the street I see the building that once housed WTOP-TV. WTOP-TV is now WUSA-TV, and has moved on to much grander quarters. I am reminded, as I have been so many times during my life, that when one door closes, others open. It may not be the door you expected to open, but if you keep moving in a direction in which you believe, things do happen. On that day, however, I truly felt that all was lost.

CHAPTER 17

OR THE NEXT SOLID YEAR, I pounded the pavement, tracking down every ad and every rumor of a job in broadcasting. On several occasions, I was told I was one of two finalists, but in the end it was one disappointment after another. One institutional radio employer told me I had the job but that some final paper clearance was necessary; then, after three months of waiting and calling, I got the word that someone else had appeared "out of the blue" with more experience than I and had been given the job. It was yet another blow. I can remember feeling depressed, angry, and not very interested in what was happening around me. I was mostly feeling sorry for myself, as well as regretful that I'd given up my position at WAMU, and I began to seriously consider going back to work as a secretary. I knew I had the necessary skills, and judging from the pages of newspaper advertisements, there were many secretarial positions available at good salaries.

In early February 1977, I met George Bauer. A former National Public Radio employee, George had just become Washington bureau chief for Physicians Radio Network (PRN), a twenty-four-hour closed-circuit broadcasting service for doctors. The content of the broadcast was actually a single hour of medical news and information, rolled over through the day and night. The operation was funded by a conglomerate of pharmaceutical companies and was based in New York City. Receivers were provided to doctors free of charge for use in their offices, to bring them the latest developments in medicine as well as advertisements for the latest prescription drugs. Interviews with specialists and feature stories on particular diseases and medical problems made up the substance of the broadcasts. The Washington office had been established to keep doctors informed of the latest news regarding government regulations and how they affected the practice of medicine.

As a regular listener to WAMU, George had heard my health-related programs, and when he began looking for a person to work with him as a correspondent for PRN, he called me. When we met, I assumed he was just picking my brain about possible medical topics to be covered in his broadcasts, but two days later he called again and asked whether I'd be interested in working with him three days a week. I was delighted. My interest in medicine was continuing to grow, and this seemed a perfect opportunity to create a specialty for myself. Within the same week, on George's recommendation, I interviewed with the managing editor of the Associated Press Radio Network about the possibility of doing freelance medical reports. He, too, had listened to my health segments, liked what he had heard, and was willing to give me a chance. So, after a year with no job, along came two in the same week.

My first day at PRN was overwhelming. Our tiny office was located in the old National Press Building, but we spent very little time there. Instead, we took microphones, cables, tapes, and tape recorders up to Capitol Hill to record a hearing on a health-related matter. I remember feeling uncomfortable and out of place sitting in a committee room in the section reserved for "press," even though I carried a pass specifying my reason for being there. It was as though I didn't truly believe I belonged, so why in the world should anyone else? Nevertheless, I listened to the proceedings intently, making notes and, at George's direction, keeping track of the counter on the tape recorder to make it easy to find any particular quote we might use in our piece. Then it was back to the Press Club, where I went over my notes and wrote a story around the bits of tape to create a five-minute piece explaining the issues. It was not an easy task. My experience up to that point had been exclusively with "live" radio, just getting on the air and talking. Now I was faced with the task of creating a report based on what I'd heard plus background material. Needless to say, that first five-minute report took many hours to complete. George Bauer was tough but encouraging, and helped me focus my thoughts.

For the Associated Press, the process was different. I used excerpts of half-hour or hour-long interviews I had done for "Mind and Body" or "Health Call," wrote copy around the excerpts, and rerecorded my own voice as narrator. The finished pieces could be no longer than sixty to ninety seconds, to be carried on AP radio stations around the country. In the early days, I was paid about ten dollars for each piece, on which I would spend at least eight hours. Of course, I got faster as the process became more familiar to me, so that eventually I could turn out a ninety-second piece in less than an hour. It was the experience and the exposure that mattered. This was a different kind of radio from what I'd been used to doing, and I was grateful for the opportunity.

Slowly I grew accustomed to going up to the Hill or to press conferences or presentations. I learned a great deal from George, developing my skills so that I could spot the key points as they were being made and have the report almost written in my head even before I returned to the office. It became a game to see just how quickly I could shape the story, record my own voice tracks, and edit the entire thing. Before I reached a point of comfort, however, there was at least one day that was horrendous. George decided to take a vacation several weeks after I'd arrived. On the Friday before he left, we went over the following week's possible stories. To begin the week, we settled on a news conference planned for Monday morning at ten, to be held in the Press Building. To be sure that I had all the necessary equipment in good operating order, I took it home with me that Friday evening and tested it out over the weekend. Then, bright and early Monday morning, I borrowed John's briefcase so that I could conveniently carry the tape recorder, cables, and microphones, and off I went, in plenty of time to arrive sufficiently early to set up my equipment before any of the principals or other members of the press arrived. There was just one problem: when I got there, the briefcase, with a combination lock, would not open.

I could not believe it. I had planned so carefully, and taken, I thought, every possible precaution to ensure that everything would be ready for my first real solo effort. I ran to a phone booth and called John's office. His secretary tracked him down at the Commerce Department and told him what the problem was. He relayed the combination to her, and I finally managed to open the briefcase. The press conference was just about to begin as I ran back into the room. With great embarrassment and perspiration dripping, I set up the microphone on the podium, which was by now crowded with many others. It was not an auspicious beginning. I was so unnerved, I could barely concentrate on the two-hour proceeding and grasp the focus of the conference. When I got back to my office, I was filled with panic. I didn't know where to begin or how to shape the story; I only knew that I had pages and pages of notes, and hours of taped material, all of which I had to condense into a five-minute report.

After I'd grappled with the material for two hours without even beginning to write the story, I once again picked up the phone and called John, and this time, luckily, he was in his office. I was so upset I could barely make myself understood. For the next forty-five minutes, he talked me through the various elements of the material. Little by little, I calmed down as he helped me clarify the major points that had to be communicated, and how best to do it. In that moment, I felt both such gratitude and such misery. I felt like a total failure, as though I were a child who simply didn't have the intellectual wherewithal to get the task done. But his encouragement and loving support helped me get through it.

In fact, part of me has come to expect a certain panic, an inner turmoil that's part of the territory when I face new challenges. I can't recall ever standing up before an audience or considering a new presentation without some measure of underlying distress. Even now, I find myself conducting something like an internal dialogue, reminding myself that I've been through many such experiences before and that I'll get through this one, too. Sometimes I say a little prayer, asking God to keep me calm and focused on what I'm doing. I gather that many actors experience many of the same feelings before a stage performance.

By the time George Bauer returned from his vacation, I had become accustomed to dealing with my sense of panic. In fact, by the end of those two weeks I realized I could manage fairly well. I spent each morning mapping out the day's activities, knowing that in the afternoon at around five o'clock the New York office would call for the feed of my recorded five-minute feature, in addition to any items of a medical or health-related nature that I could contribute to the daily newscast. As much as I had dreaded the prospect of functioning on my own, I became accustomed to juggling the various activities that were expected of me. For the first time, I began to feel as though I was up to the task.

I learned a lot during my two years with PRN. First and foremost, I learned not to let the big networks overwhelm me. One of my tactics was to make sure I got to each event an hour ahead of time so that I could set up my microphone on the podium before anyone else arrived. Otherwise, there would be no room, because the networks and other broadcasters would crowd out those of us from smaller organizations. I learned to listen as carefully to what was asked by reporters as I did to what was offered by officials. I learned how to make my way toward the front of the room instead of hanging back; that way, I'd have more of a chance to be called on when it was time for questions. And I learned to rely on my own judgment. Since George and I usually went our separate ways to cover different stories, it was important that I depend less and less on him and more on myself. Except for the fact that I sometimes had to get out of bed as early as 4:30 a.m. and to carry heavy loads of equipment, I was beginning to enjoy myself.

CHAPTER 18

IN JUNE 1979, after I'd been with Physicians Radio Network for two years, I received a telephone call from Irma Aandahl, who told me that her husband was retiring from his position at the State Department and that the two of them were moving to Princeton, New Jersey. She wanted me to know, she said, because that meant there would be an opening for her position as host of "Kaleidoscope." Even though I'd gone on doing my two health programs for the station on a volunteer basis throughout my two-year stint at PRN and was at the station at least once every week, I'd had no idea she might be leaving. She told me the job would be advertised and filled after an extensive country-wide search, and that she, personally, would have no part in choosing her successor.

I wasn't at all sure I wanted to apply for the host's spot. First of all, it was a full-time position. I had grown quite happy and comfortable with a three-day-a-week schedule because it afforded me a great deal of flexibility, allowing me to spend more time with our children and also to travel with John. We'd taken several trips during my time at PRN and I'd enjoyed a sense of freedom. Also, I'd been concentrating on medicine and health-related issues for two years and was unsure about broadening my focus. The three-hour morning program that Irma had hosted for ten years focused on a wide range of topics and would require a very different approach. I also learned that the program would be cut back to two hours because NPR was planning to introduce a new daily program in November, "Morning Edition," to be broadcast from 6:00 a.m. to 10:00 a.m.

I went home that evening to consider whether to apply for the position and to talk it over with John. Once again, I hesitated to put myself on the line. After all, there seemed very little likelihood that the station, under the auspices of American University, would hire someone for a full-time position who was not a college graduate. That seemed especially relevant because I knew that the host of one of the other weekly programs at WAMU, a Harvard graduate with a master's in education, was also interested in the job. Once again, I was plagued by my anxieties.

At John's urging, I made up a list of pluses and minuses, both in terms of what it would mean to give up my current part-time position for a full-time job and also in terms of what it would mean to me personally to go after the host's position. There was a salary differential: I would be paid exactly the same amount for five days at WAMU as I was being paid for three days at PRN. Of course, I would receive benefits (health and life insurance, plus sick leave, vacation pay, and the opportunity to take courses at AU) that I didn't enjoy in my current position. I must have agonized over that list for a full week before I finally decided to go for it. I can't say that there was any one deciding factor, other than that the challenge of broadening my horizon seemed more appealing than the notion of continuing to specialize. Despite my doubts about myself, I've always had within me a desire to put myself out there on the edge.

Once I had submitted the application, the wait seemed interminable. I learned that about a hundred people from all over the country had applied, and that knowledge further dimmed my hopes. I felt sure there were talented people with far more experience than I had ready and willing to step into the job. The friends I talked with about my application were all encouraging, but it was hard to listen to them; their views seemed so unrealistic when measured against my absolute conviction that I couldn't get the job. I heard from people within the office that the other in-house candidate, the one with the degree from Harvard, was convinced that she would get the position and was already making plans to reshape the show.

Finally, on a sunny August morning, WAMU's program director, Michael Nitka, asked me to come into his office. I hadn't slept much the night before, because I knew the decision was coming. In addition, John was out of the country, which heightened my unease. I braced myself for what I was sure would be polite words of rejection. And then the magic happened. Mike said, "So how would you like to come to work full-time for WAMU as the host of 'Kaleidoscope'?" I couldn't believe it! I managed to say I'd be thrilled, and with a quaky, teary voice said I would do absolutely everything I could to maintain the high quality the station had grown accustomed to with Irma as host. I left his office floating on air, afraid that I might scream out to the whole world, "I got it!"

The frustration was that I couldn't share the news with John. He was in Geneva, Switzerland, at the time, working at a frantic pace on negotiations for a trade agreement. By the time he called several days later, I had arrived at a calmer assessment of my achievement, so I didn't blurt out the news immediately. Finally, about a third of the way into the conversation, he remembered that I'd been waiting for the decision and asked whether I'd heard anything. I said in a quite normal voice, "As a matter of fact, I got the job." Across the transatlantic line came a whoop of delight and pleasure. I think I had so discouraged both of us from thinking I might get it that he was really surprised. It was quite a moment.

During the same year, Jennie became a five-day boarder at Madeira School in McLean, Virginia, and David was a freshman at Oberlin, so my days as a chauffeuring mother were over. Jennie told us later how much she loved those years in high school because, she said, she felt like a "princess," with her parents happy to see her on weekends but without the "hassle" of having to deal with us during the week. The two kids seemed genuinely pleased that I'd gotten the job, though several years later, when the name of the program was changed to "The Diane Rehm Show," I think they felt a certain loss of privacy.

CHAPTER 19

MY FIRST DAY on the air as the official host of "Kaleidoscope" was Tuesday, September 4, 1979. Of course, I had been at the studio for many days before that, looking over scripts, getting ideas from people about what they saw as the strengths and weaknesses of the program, and familiarizing myself with the day-to-day requirements. I had no intention of bringing any major change to the format; it seemed to me that listeners had grown happily accustomed to hearing the program in its current form for ten years. Adjusting to a new host would be difficult enough. I understood that people often become extraordinarily attached to radio personalities, and that I shouldn't do anything drastic that might underscore the fact that Irma was gone and I was taking her place. I had heard the callers who'd phoned in to tell Irma how much they would miss her, people who had actually cried on her last day on the air.

Those early days are painful to recall. As much as I hoped I was prepared for the challenge of moving into Irma's chair, my body reacted with a vengeance. No matter what I ate, I suffered from chronic diarrhea. At first, I thought it was a symptom of a virus of some kind that would eventually disappear, and I was embarrassed to talk about the problem with anyone, even my husband or a doctor. I thought I could deal with it and make it go away. There were days when, upon arriving at the studio, I would sit in the car trying to quiet my mind and my body, willing my insides to cease and desist. In fact, the problem lasted for nine months. I lost ten pounds during that period, and probably looked as bad as I felt. I've always thought that you can't fool the body. I might have wanted to believe that I was coping with my anxiety, performing well on the air, bringing in the right guests, asking the right questions, and generally moving the program along on the right track, but deep down I was literally consumed by doubts. Even though I'd gotten the job and was receiving great encouragement from the station's top echelon, part of me felt that those who'd made the decision to hire me had made a mistake. I've come to recognize that there are a great many people who feel this way, both men and women, but especially women. Time and energy are spent reminding yourself that you're not just pretending to be who or what you are, that you really do have what it takes to do the job you've been given. If I could retrieve all the hours I've spent stewing in self-doubt, I'd surely be a much younger woman. I try to believe there's some advantage to this kind of thinking—it does make you try harder than if you were completely confident in your skills and talents. The way I went about it could certainly be regarded as overpreparing.

From my first day on the air, I made sure I knew what I was talking about. That meant hours of preparation, preparation involving talking ahead of time with each guest, reading background material, making notes for use on the air, and in general gathering sufficient information to make me comfortable. So on that first day when I was seated in the host's chair, I invited Hobart Rowen, economics columnist for the *Washington Post*, to be my guest. I'd always admired the clarity and incisiveness of his writing, and there were numerous issues I wanted to discuss with him. Since my husband's legal specialty was international trade, I had some familiarity with matters relating to economics and felt I could hold my own. The subject that morning was "The Chrysler Crunch," examining the issues that had led to the corporation's current difficulties. Bart was just as charming and likable in person as his columns were lucid, and I was pleased that I had invited him to participate.

I think what gratified me the most as time went on was the willingness of people like Bart to appear as guests on the program. I would read articles about some fascinating national or international issue, note the names mentioned, pick up the phone and call them, and was quite often happily surprised when they agreed to come on. This was, of course, in the early days of talk radio, and there weren't many outlets for discussion of serious issues. When the comet Kohoutek first came into view, for example, one of the people frequently quoted was Dr. Richard Berendzen, a physicist then with the National Academy of Science, who was happy to appear on the program. Another cooperative guest early in my career was Madeleine Albright, then president of the Center for National Policy. Her knowledge and understanding of foreign affairs was stunning, and the ease with which she was able to communicate even the most complex issues made her one of our most reliable experts. It was no surprise to me when President Clinton appointed her first as U.S. ambassador to the United Nations and later as the first female secretary of state. The secretary once said to a large gathering that "Diane had me on her show when I was a nobody." My response to that was and is, Madeleine Albright was never a nobody!

I've come to know various talk-show hosts over the years, and their approaches vary. Larry King is the prime example of one who doesn't believe in reading the books of the authors he interviews, preferring to ask the kind of spontaneous questions an uninformed listener might pose. My own belief is that both listener and author benefit from having an informed interviewer. There are a great many questions I might ask spontaneously that would be less interesting and less informative than those that spring from my reading of a book or other material prepared for me. But Larry is a great host. For many years he earned his title as the "king of talk radio" before he gave it up to move to CNN.

Guests appreciated my efforts to be an informed interviewer and often expressed their gratitude. There were, however, a few notable exceptions. One was Tony Randall. I'd been contacted by the Wolf Trap Farm Park theater in suburban Virginia where the star of stage, screen, and television was to appear, asking if I would care to interview him. I had seen him occasionally on the television program "The Odd Couple" and thought that listeners would enjoy hearing him, so I readily agreed and we set a date for the interview. When Mr. Randall arrived at the studio, there was great excitement. Up to that point, we'd had few celebrities, and the staff was eager to see him and listen to the interview as I was taping it. He seemed somewhat aloof when we were introduced, but I assumed he'd be more forthcoming once the interview was under way. The two of us sat down in the recording studio, and the staff gathered with the engineer in his adjoining area. Before we began, I asked Mr. Randall whether there was anything in particular he'd like to discuss during the interview. He looked at me with a smirk on his face and said, "Well, you might want to ask me about the size of my cock." The staff burst into loud guffaws, which he couldn't hear but which I was aware of because I could see through the glass separating the engineer from the recording studio. I managed to keep my cool, but it took a lot of effort on my part because I was absolutely livid with anger. If I were confronted with that kind of behavior today, I would simply walk out, but insecure as I was, I went on with the interview, which was totally uninspired and lackluster. When it was over, after the engineer had turned off the microphones and as Randall was leaving the studio, he slapped himself on the forehead and exclaimed, "Oh my God, we didn't talk about my appearance at Wolf Trap!" This time it was my turn to smile and say, "Don't worry about it, Mr. Randall. I'll take care of it." And take care of it I did. The interview never aired.

Why did he do what he did? Who knows. Perhaps he was amused by the sight of a nervous, uptight woman and thought it might be fun to be outlandishly provocative. Perhaps he reverted to adolescence as he played to the audience of young men and women in the engineer's studio. Maybe he was annoyed about having to take the time to promote his appearance at Wolf Trap. Perhaps he just thought he was being funny. More likely is the possibility that he himself was somewhat nervous about the interview and thought his strategy would be sufficiently unnerving to throw me off-balance. I read recently that at seventy-three, he'd become the father of a baby girl. I hope he's found the maturity to treat that child with respect.

CHAPTER 20

*E*VEN AS I BECAME more and more involved in my work, I didn't regard what I was doing as a "career." My background didn't allow me to think of myself in that way. Rather, I was a woman with a husband and two children who happened to have a job in radio. Though I was dedicated to doing the best work I could, I hadn't reached a point where I was thinking about how I might advance professionally. After all, I kept reminding myself, I'd had no real training other than my apprenticeship and on-the-job experience. I saw myself as someone who had lucked into a job, and, for that reason, still felt like something of a fraud. When *The Cinderella Complex* was published, a book talking about the number of women who thought of themselves as great pretenders, I could identify with those feelings.

I needed a lot of help during this period, and so I returned to therapy. Slowly, with a pastoral counselor, Maxine Thornton

Denham, I began once again to confront those feelings of insecurity and inferiority that had been with me all my life. She listened patiently, gently encouraging me to probe the underlying messages I was sending to myself. They were messages of anger and disappointment—blaming, accusatory messages, aimed at both John and myself. Of course, learning that old tapes are running in your head doesn't necessarily shut down the tape recorder. First there had to come a conscious awareness that those old voices were repeating the same negative messages to me, a very difficult task. Again and again, the internal tapes were saying, "You can't do it. You're a failure. Your choices are wrong. You don't articulate well. Your questions are silly." Though a listener might have felt that a given show was worthwhile and my questions relevant, I was a harsh critic of myself and of John. Consequently, I had to break the pattern of allowing those voices to dictate to me, to respond to them with a vigorous internal dialogue that would counter the negativity.

Much of this dialogue had to do with my mother. The more I allowed myself to realize how conflicted I was in my feelings toward her, the sadder and angrier I became. I could scarcely think of her without feeling both desolate and hostile, as though she were still a constant and active part of my life. In fact, my mother has been dead for more than forty years now, but the feelings of childhood helplessness I experienced in her presence have remained with me to this day. People who've never been through therapy may have a hard time understanding both how difficult and how effective it can be to bring long-buried issues to the surface. In fact, others stronger than I might argue, Why bother? But for me, the acknowledgment to myself that I was struggling to free myself of a lifelong burden was a crucial first step, one that allowed me to grapple with the destructive feelings that had been part of my life for so many years.

Intermingled with my feelings about my mother were questions and doubts about my marriage. Though John and I could acknowledge to each other the differences in our upbringing and approach to issues, that awareness didn't free us from frequent quarrels about anything and everything, but mostly about my perception that I didn't have a fully participating partner. John's usual response was to withdraw, to refrain from speaking for days or weeks. He preferred not to deal with whatever the problem was rather than to face me directly. Slowly, through my anger, I came to understand that I was experiencing the same feelings I'd had as a child when my mother rejected me. To my horror, I began to believe that, in some ways, I'd actually married a man who behaved just the way she did. Then, of course, the question became, did I marry him *because* he behaved just as my mother did, or was it simply my misfortune to have come upon a man with similar behavior patterns? It was a frightening question.

Perhaps in some ways I had sought out the very characteristics in John that I had encountered in my mother because they were familiar. When I read about child abuse cases, my heart goes out to the youngster who, despite horrendous parental treatment, longs to be reunited with that parent. I understand very well the longing for the familiar, no matter how dangerous. The same holds true for the abused wife who risks everything by refusing to allow police to remove an abusive spouse from a life-threatening situation, in part because she fears a loss of financial support but also because she may need to stay with this man almost because his abuse is a known factor. In our case, there was never any physical abuse, but I do regard what went on between us intermittently as psychologically abusive behavior. We both engaged in it. On the other hand, there were periods of enormous closeness, both physical and emotional, when we expressed our love for each other and our commitment to the marriage. The times of reconciliation were wonderful, when we could laugh together, express our passion, and do all the things that had drawn us together in the first place.

It was during this very period of ups and downs that we

embarked on a series of radio programs together, about marriage and family issues. When I first broached the idea with my program director and supervisor, he thought it was a good one. The plan was that John and I would choose a general topic, outline it in our own minds (without sharing our ideas with each other), and then simply go into the studio and start talking, off the cuff. As host of the program, I would introduce John, give listeners an idea of what we hoped to cover in the hour, and invite them to participate with their own experiences or questions. For our first topic we chose "What Happens When Wives Return to Work?" I remember how proud I felt the first time as John sat across from the table from me in the old studios of WAMU. After all, we really didn't know how it would work, what each of us might say, what our own reactions might be, or how the listening audience might respond. That first program was broadcast after we'd been married for twenty-two years. David was twenty-one, Jennie seventeen.

I introduced the first program by citing the fact that 50 percent of the nation's married women were working or looking for work, and by saying that we hoped to talk about the adjustments to change that had come about in our own lives as a result of my shift from the home into the workplace. John began by talking about his expectations when we first married, his assumption that I would be a somewhat conventional housewife. He regarded himself as an ardent supporter of feminism, but once I began volunteering at the radio station and later took a paid position, he realized he felt an ambivalence. He assumed that my work life wouldn't really entail much change in our home life. What that meant, in fact, was that he expected that I would more or less continue with the same activities and responsibilities that I had carried out before my "working life" began. (For the record, I feel that homemakers are among the hardest-working people in our society. Unfortunately, they don't receive a salary for all they do.) For example, he said, "Diane used to do a lovely job of ironing my shirts and I love freshly ironed shirts. She doesn't do them anymore. Her job obviously began to interfere with the kind and the amount of cooking that she could do." And then came an even more personal statement. He said, "Getting down to more significant aspects of the changing relationship, I can certainly recall a few years ago when, while my law practice was certainly going well, it didn't have anything particularly dramatic about it, and I saw Diane's career clearly on the rise. I have to admit now, which I don't think I admitted to myself then, that that caused feelings of genuine envy and insecurity on my part that somehow I was sort of just moving along in a fairly even fashion and Diane's meteor was really taking off. That was not easy to deal with at the time." It was quite an admission on John's part, and one that got us talking about many things, both small and large. This was in 1981, so John and I were clearly ahead of the curve in our struggle with these issues of equity in the home, issues about which books are being written today.

We went on to do subsequent programs about money in marriage (I related the checkbook incident on the air and John confessed to just how upset he'd been at the loss of the control), religion in marriage (we discussed his resistance to becoming part of the church community), dependence and independence in marriage, and holiday celebrations. During the program on "Dependence and Independence," we had a surprise caller on the air. David Rehm phoned in from Oberlin, where he was attending college, to say, "I just want you both to know that, whether you're together or whether you're apart, I love you both very much." I daresay it was a powerful and emotional moment, not only for us but for our audience. Longtime listeners of the program still remind me of that incredible display of support from our son.

Unbelievably, there were times just prior to an already announced upcoming program when we weren't even speaking to each other. I know how strange that sounds, but we were both determined to go on with the show despite our difficulties. And invariably, doing the program got us out of our slump. Something happened to the two of us during those hours when we knew that no matter what had gone on just before, we were a team. My boss regarded the series as a hit and encouraged us to do more programs. Listeners wrote in to tell us that they were using our tapes to try to solve problems in their own marriages. One woman wrote to tell me that several couples in her neighborhood had joined together to listen to each tape and engage in group discussion afterward. There were many requests for cassette copies of those programs, and John and I have always remembered that series with pride.

Those programs, however, did not bring an end to our periodic estrangements. It was not until years later, during an extended period of counseling with a third therapist, Jack Harris, that I finally came to understand that when impulses toward separation and withdrawal came over John, rather than attempt to woo him back, I had to move farther away from him. At first, this seemed counterintuitive, and was perhaps the hardest learning I faced in my emotional maturation process. It was a major turning point, one that granted me a new sense of freedom and independence and allowed me to avoid the yearning and self-pity that had accompanied our periods of emotional separation for so many years. And it was clear that it worked. Whenever I would move away from him as he went into those periods of separation, he would return more quickly.

There was another significant event that occurred during this period. John and I were having a particularly difficult time, so I decided to go off with a good friend for a few days to get away from the tension. She and I decided to drive to a resort about three hours away to swim, play tennis, walk, talk, and just relax. At the same time, John had gone to New York to deal with a client's problem and then take his mother to lunch. In the morning, as he was walking along to meet his mother, without quite knowing why, he stopped in at St. Thomas Episcopal Church on

Fifth Avenue. He told me later that as he sat there thinking about the extent to which he had resisted Christ, he was overcome by a mixture of grief and joy, and he began to weep uncontrollably. He sat there in a pew for more than an hour, struggling with his feelings for me, for the life we had together, for our children, but, most of all, for Christ.

It was a life-changing experience for him. When he came home, he called me to try to explain what had happened. As soon as I heard his voice, I became alarmed. He sounded almost as though he'd had a nervous breakdown. Though he was articulate, I had never heard him express himself with this kind of emotionality, crying as he told me how much he loved me and begging for a chance to prove his dedication to our marriage. He asked me to cut short my trip and come home as soon as possible, but I decided to wait at least another day. I wanted to think about all he'd said and talk with him again the next day. When I hung up the phone, I explained to my friend what had happened and we both decided to return to Washington two days earlier than scheduled.

That event did indeed change John's life. He decided to be baptized in the Episcopal church, with Jane Dixon acting as his godmother and David Busby standing in as his godfather. A year later, he began work on a master's degree in theological studies at Wesley Theological Seminary, not far from our home. Continuing with his law practice, he took only one course a semester, doing his studying and writing his papers at night and on weekends. After five years, he had completed only half the work necessary to earn the master's, so he applied for and was granted a five-year extension, after a great deal of debate on the part of the faculty. It was the first time in the seminary's history that a student had been permitted to take ten years to complete a master's. All of our family and friends celebrated at his graduation, understanding the remarkable journey he had traveled to reach this point. In fact, some of his partners worried that he might carry on with his studies and go into the ministry full-time, but that was never part of his plan.

CHAPTER 21

*D*ESPITE MY ONGOING feelings of insecurity, I began to feel physically and mentally stronger, and with that strength came a sense of wanting to move forward with the program, to try innovations. In particular, I wanted to enlarge the program's political dimension. Until then, the focus had been on listeners, primarily female, who were at home, but by 1980, with greater numbers of automobiles coming out of the factory equipped with FM radios, it was clear that our listenership had expanded to include commuters. Many of these were men moving around the area by car, tuning in to what was then identified as "talk programming." Little by little, I began to move away from topics that might be primarily of interest to women toward those that would be of equal interest to men.

I made changes gradually, in part out of what seemed to me appropriate caution and in part out of loyalty to Irma and her inspiration. She was a woman with such a formidable educational-radio background that I was loath to turn away from her guidance and direction. In fact, it was not until early 1984, five full years after I'd assumed the host position, that I finally realized I was tired of—in truth, almost bored with—what I was doing. My program director at the time, Craig Oliver, was wise enough to recognize that what I needed was a shift in emphasis. So together we began to create a new format, one that allowed me the freedom to choose from a wider range of topics and to place greater emphasis on politics and news stories. It was an era when political activity was becoming more intense, especially with the growth of the religious right during the Reagan years. The line between liberal and conservative thought was increasingly becoming sharply defined, and I yearned to include conversations on the program that would help crystallize the debates taking place in the halls of Congress, the White House, the courts, and the various branches of government.

It was also at this same time, in July 1984, that the program was renamed. Up until then, "Kaleidoscope" had been fine with me. But as the number of talk programs around the country increased, identification became very much host-centered. That meant that people tuned in to a program not only because of the subject matter but also because they knew they'd be hearing a particular person on the air each day, someone whose voice they recognized and whose views they could identify with. And so "The Diane Rehm Show" came into being. It was my idea, and I felt bold making this suggestion, but Craig agreed immediately. Having my name associated with the program was different from being known as the host of "Kaleidoscope." Now there was a sense of a single person related to the program, one who had a name and a presence on the air for two hours each day. I had come to realize that the name of the host, if different from the program name, was forgettable, but that the person whose name was attached to the program became a full-fledged human being in the mind of the listener. There has always been, and continues to be, debate on this point, especially in public radio. While commercial talk shows are, for the most part, associated with a particular person, the argument in public radio has been that the show should not be host-driven. But in 1984, naming the WAMU show for the host seemed just right.

It came at the right time for me personally as well. I was ready for the program to reflect more of my own ideas and interests. I wanted it to be a rich mixture of politics, science, the economy, education, the arts, and music. With increasing frequency, we were able to attract prominent guests to the program. John was outwardly supportive, but I think the name change of the program, because it brought more attention to me and a greater numbers of listeners, made it somewhat more difficult for him. People began to say things to him like "How does it feel to be the husband of Diane Rehm?" or "Your wife is so wonderful. You're a lucky man." He would respond affirmatively in public, but privately the strain between us was growing. Even our friends noticed a difference in him. The greater the attention that was focused on me, the more extended the periods of silence between us became. To a certain extent, I think David and Jennie were uncomfortable with the name recognition they received because of my program, feeling it was intruding on their privacy. When the time came for college, both decided on schools away from the East Coast.

The program took on its new name and new sound (complete with new music: I finally felt free to leave behind Irma's "Kaleidoscope" introductory theme). After weeks of planning and testing, we introduced the new format, which included three different topics in the first hour and a single subject in the second hour. The theory was to bring the sound of the program more into line with that of "Morning Edition" from National Public Radio, the program that preceded it. Looking back at the subjects for that first week, I'm overwhelmed by the thought of how much preparation it required. For example, on Monday, July 9,

1984, at 10:00 a.m., I spoke with a young woman about Maryland's automobile lemon law. At 10:30, Andrei Sakharov was my guest. At 11:00 a.m., I interviewed an author, Fred Powledge, about his book called *Fat of the Land*. On Tuesday of that week, I spoke with *Washington Post* columnist Richard Cohen about the prospects of a woman for vice president in the 1984 election, had a discussion about child abuse with psychologist Stanley Katz, and conducted a segment with whistle-blower Ernest Fitzgerald about waste in Air Force spending. In the second hour, at 11:00 a.m., the topic was "Children of Interracial Marriages," with three panelists. The week went on at the same pace: two or three subjects in the first hour, with the second hour devoted to a single topic. Looking back today, I can't imagine how I did it all. I was calling prospective guests, booking, researching, writing, and, finally, interviewing all of these people on all of these subjects every single day, with only a part-time volunteer assistant. It was not only exhausting, it was crazy! There were times during that period when I'd leave for the office at seven-thirty in the morning and wouldn't return before seven-thirty or eight in the evening. I was giving my all to the program, in part because the station had little money and was unwilling to hire a part- or full-time producer for me, and also because working so hard gave me the satisfaction I didn't experience at home. I continued to push hard for an assistant, however, refusing to accept the idea that WAMU couldn't afford to allocate money for a producer. I knew that the only way to get action on this was to raise the issue again and again, to try to get WAMU's new manager to understand its importance to the station as well as to me personally.

One of the changes I made in the program after it became "The Diane Rehm Show" was to institute a Friday roundup of the week's top news stories. I began this with just two journalists, who alternated each week. The first was John Wallach of Hearst Newspapers, and the second was Simon Hoggert, a British journalist then writing for the *Times* of London. John has since left

Hearst to establish Seeds of Peace, an organization devoted to bringing Palestinian and Israeli youth together each year for a period of several weeks. Then we expanded the roundup to include three journalists, making it a lively discussion among people with different approaches, covering numerous topics from activities in Congress, the White House, and domestic politics to foreign affairs. At first, my supervisor argued against bringing in more than one journalist at a time, believing that a single voice would be more effective and easier to comprehend. But I felt that mixing reporters from different publications would offer listeners a variety of ideas and allow them to hear how journalists covering the same subjects could reach vastly different conclusions. The "Friday News Roundup" has become our most popular hour of the week.

In addition to covering current news stories, I reserved the second hour for longer, more in-depth interviews. One very special conversation occurred in 1985, when the actress Liv Ullmann came for an interview. Her appointment as special ambassador for UNICEF had taken her to desolate spots all over the world, where she reached out to hungry and dying children. Her book called *Choices* had just been published, so we discussed both her life and her work. She talked about how much acting meant to her, but I had the sense that she cared very little for stardom. She seemed a very private person, allowing herself to express her deepest thoughts only through the printed word. I'll never forget looking across the table at that beautiful face with its flawless skin and pale blue eyes brimming with tears as she recalled the sickness and misery she'd encountered on her travels. Knowing that she'd recently ended her relationship with the Swedish film director Ingmar Bergman, I found it amazing that any man could let her go. Given her worldwide fame as a star of stage and screen, I kept wondering what it was that had motivated her to expose herself to the disease and deprivation of the Third World, and whether she was moved somehow to make up for the kind of privileges she herself had enjoyed. She revealed only that she felt compassion for those who were starving and believed she could use her position to draw attention to their plight.

Two years later, I met Audrey Hepburn, who had taken on the special UN position for UNICEF for that year. Her own motivation, considering her experience of hunger and danger during World War II, seemed far more understandable. All during my twenties and thirties, Audrey Hepburn had been the epitome of elegance. Her clothes, her posture, her manner of speaking, all conveyed a perfection that one could only dream of possessing. Yet here she was in my studio, fully human, warm, kind, and painfully thin. The dark shadows under her eyes seemed to represent more than ordinary fatigue. She seemed physically fragile, yet she spoke with strength and fervor about the help needed for the young people living in dire circumstances in poor countries around the world. Neither she nor Liv Ullmann demonstrated anything other than warmth and a genuine passion for what they were doing. I never for a moment believed they had lent their efforts to be used merely as "faces" on a poster. Fine actresses, yes, but also caring human beings who brought intelligence and determination to their task.

Unfortunately, the prominent guests weren't all as appealing as Liv Ullmann or Audrey Hepburn. A year after interviewing Hepburn, I was faced with a discomfiting situation, and this time, with the assistance of listeners, I rose to the challenge. Tom Clancy was already a best-selling author (*Red Storm Rising* and *The Hunt for Red October*) by the time I met him in 1986. I was on the air doing the first hour of the program when he arrived at the studio with an escort. When I finally went out to the lobby to greet him, I thought it somewhat odd that he hadn't removed his aviator sunglasses. When I guided him into the studio and he still didn't take them off, I simply assumed that he was in the habit of wearing them all the time. However, as we waited through the NPR newscast to go on the air, he propped his elbow on the table and shielded his eyes completely. In other words, he chose not to look directly at me. As the newscast ended and the interview began, Clancy's posture did not change. He kept his arm propped on his elbow, with his hand shading his eyes. His head was tilted downward, so he was looking down at the table. I read my introduction, invited listeners to call, and then asked my first question, a fairly open-ended one to give him a chance to respond as fully as possible. To my surprise, he gave me a one-word answer (either a yes or a no, I can't remember which). So I threw out a second question, equally broad and intended to elicit a full-bodied response, but to my dismay, a single-word response (or, as I recall, something more like a grunt) ensued. As much as I tried, this man was not going to engage in a conversation with me.

After about fifteen minutes of this painful nondialogue, I realized I had two options. I could say to him and to my listeners that it seemed clear to me that he didn't wish to be interviewed and invite him to leave. Or I could open the phones; perhaps, I reasoned, he might display a different attitude in response to listeners' questions. I chose the second route, and to my delight, the first caller (male) took care of the whole problem for me. He began by saying how much he'd enjoyed reading Clancy's books, and how wonderful a writer he believed Clancy to be. "But," he went on, "I have to tell you, Mr. Clancy, you sure are sounding arrogant this morning in your interview with Diane." For the first time, Tom Clancy sat up at attention and removed his glasses. "Why, what do you mean?" he asked. "Diane and I are getting along just fine, aren't we, Diane?" Before I could respond, the caller jumped in. "That's not the way it sounds to me, Mr. Clancy. You're giving her one-word answers to very good questions, and not being very forthcoming." At this point, Clancy seemed to squirm, then uttered a halfhearted apology for sounding as though he wasn't cooperating, but he assured the caller that he was enjoying the interview and found me an engaging talk-show host. (That was certainly news to me!) The comments of the first caller were echoed by those of subsequent callers, and from that point on, Clancy was a pussycat. It was the first, but not the last, time listeners came to my rescue.

A similar incident occurred when Margaret Truman Daniel came on the show to plug her latest mystery. She seemed bored and out of sorts and would barely respond to my questions. I considered bringing the interview to a premature end, but once again, especially out of respect for her as the daughter of our late president, I decided to open the phones, and again listeners came through for me, telling her how much they admired her father but criticizing her for her attitude on the air. She was clearly taken aback, and perked up immediately. The audience is an extraordinary group of people, who listen carefully, not only to substance but to nuance. They know exactly what's going on, and how to deal with what they see as a problem. That was the first and last time I ever had Tom Clancy and Margaret Truman Daniel on the program. Various publicists have since called me on their behalf, but being burned once was enough for me.

There were other very different experiences to counter those I had with Tom Clancy and Margaret Truman Daniel. In 1986, I received a paperback edition of a book called *Race Hoss: Big Emma's Boy*. It was an autobiographical account of the life of Albert "Race" Sample, a black man who had served seventeen years in the Texas prison system. His mother, "Big Emma," had been a prostitute and a bootlegger, using Albert as both a pimp and a lookout for her, starting at age four. She both loved and hated him, because he was the product of her relationship with a white man. His skin was quite light in color, and she constantly ridiculed him because of it, calling him "Peckerwood." When she was arrested for bootlegging and cheating at cards, she was sent to jail, and he was placed in a cell with her. Emma screamed and cried and hollered so loudly she was finally released, only to be chased out of town by the Ku Klux Klan. This time, she left four-year-old Albert behind to fend for himself. Albert grew up on the streets, begging for food and money, hiding from police and truant officers, never giving up faith that Emma would someday return for him. When she finally did, Albert was a streetwise teenager who could no longer tolerate his mother's bullying, so he went off on his own. He got into a number of scrapes with police, however, and a judge told him he had to go into the service or he would spend a lifetime in prison.

Albert took the judge's advice and joined the army, but after his service, he returned to the life he knew and began committing robberies, eventually ending up in Retrieve, a prison with a reputation for brutal treatment, after being convicted of armed robbery. He spent seventeen years there, and the stories he told about life in that institution were almost unbelievable. One in particular had to do with the murder of a younger man by his older lover after he learned of his unfaithfulness. The older man had a butcher knife, and with one swift stroke, according to Race Hoss, cut off the younger man's head, which then rolled onto the floor of the cafeteria during the dinner hour. The entire group of prisoners who witnessed the event simply ignored it.

Race Hoss's story has a happy ending. After he was released from prison for good behavior, he got a job working for a local newspaper. Eventually, the editor offered him a chance to write about his time in prison, and he wrote several columns about conditions at Retrieve. The Texas governor read the pieces, asked to meet him, and ultimately invited him to join his staff to establish a job placement service for inmates coming out of prison. Race Hoss worked successfully at that for several years before taking on other government jobs. He now lives quietly in Austin with his wife, Carol. He and I both wept during that interview, one of the most moving I've ever participated in. Each year around Christmas, I rebroadcast our conversation, and always receive hundreds of requests for cassette copies.

Several years ago, former president Jimmy Carter came in for his third interview with me, this one relating to his autobiography.

In it, he talked about his regret at having made so many decisions without first consulting or confiding in his wife, Rosalynn. He spoke of the difficult periods in their marriage, and how, on at least one occasion, they had prayed together to help them become better partners. At that moment in the conversation, I took a risk. I said, "Mr. President, was there ever a time when you and Mrs. Carter seriously considered divorce?" He looked at me, and then looked down at the table, pausing for as much as ten seconds, as I wondered whether he would answer the question or simply ignore it. When he finally spoke, there were tears in his eyes. He said, "Yes, Diane, we did consider divorce. It was a very difficult time for both of us, but we managed to get through it." He told me afterward that he had never before made that statement publicly but felt he had to answer my question honestly.

Someone asked me the other day whether talking with some of the world's outstanding figures didn't leave me starstruck. I acknowledge that my place behind the microphone affords me an opportunity few people in this world enjoy, that is, to spend an hour—alone—with people like these. I know how fortunate I've been to have had that opportunity and to have had the vast majority of guests, no matter how extraordinary, treat me with simple kindness and respect. Which brings me to a point in which I believe very strongly: you get what you give in this business. If you treat guests, listeners, and colleagues with respect, they will, almost without exception, treat you in the same way. There have been many times on the air when I could have responded angrily to the comments of a guest or caller, and believe me, there have been many times when I've wanted to. Perhaps that kind of outburst might have been entertaining, and numerous talk-show hosts around the country do use their guests as foils for their aggressive humor. I've chosen to move in a different direction. I have a hard time listening to that kind of harshness on the air, which is no doubt why it's not part of my approach to broadcasting.

People tell me they admire my ability to "keep my cool" in

the face of hostile behavior by an occasional caller, and they ask how I do it. The answer is fairly simple. First of all, it happens extremely rarely. People who call in to the program know that it's a show that produces quality guests and, in turn, expects quality callers. Second, I know I'm in control. I have my hand on a lever that allows me to "fade" down a caller who becomes obstreperous or too long-winded, and even press a button that immediately takes the caller off the air. In extreme circumstances, when a caller utters a four-letter word or makes an absolutely outrageous statement that is so provocative it shouldn't be on the air, I have a seven-second delay mechanism that either the engineer or I can activate. Without sounding at all flustered or impolite, I can respond calmly and forthrightly. Now, if that person were in my face, I think my behavior might be somewhat different. Control is absolutely necessary for my comfort on the air. I know it's why I can seem so calm, and I know that my engineers are there to back me up. If they hear something and I don't react quickly enough, they can also take that person off the air. So it's really a no-lose situation.

At times when discussions among guests in the studio become overly heated, I'll raise both my hands and jump in very loudly. In extreme situations, I'll motion to the engineer to cut off the offending guest's microphone. I took that action some years ago, when participants on opposing sides of a program on gun control got out of hand. They were yelling at each other at the same time, so listeners could barely understand what either was saying. Most of the time, I tend to use a fairly soft but stern voice to settle things down, but that was one occasion when my voice had to rise above theirs. I've since learned that with subjects as controversial as gun control, abortion rights, or the Middle East, it's much more sensible to give each guest a separate half hour than to put them in the studio together.

CHAPTER 22

IN EARLY 1988, I had the good fortune to interview
John O'Toole, the executive producer of a program
broadcast on public television called "Modern Maturity."
Geared to those aged fifty and older, the program was under-
written by the American Association of Retired Persons (AARP)
and focused on aging as a lifetime process. "You're always
involved in it," O'Toole was fond of saying. "As you get into it
more personally, you're somebody's mother, then somebody's
grandmother, and so on." Shortly after his appearance on my
program, O'Toole called to ask whether I'd be interested in
serving as a correspondent for "Modern Maturity" during the
1988 primary election campaign. The idea certainly interested
me, but after my earlier experience, I was unsure whether I
could do television. The other troubling factor was that a fair
amount of travel was involved, to Iowa and Florida to interview
older voters on their views on the candidates and the campaign.

O'Toole assured me that the producers he was assigning to the project were very experienced and would assist me in any way necessary. He also understood my reluctance to abandon my radio program, however temporarily, to conduct the interviews out of town, so he scheduled them for weekends.

It was an exciting but exhausting period. I would finish my show at noon on Friday, head for the airport, meet the TV crew, and fly out to Des Moines or Miami, memorizing my scripts along the way. In each city, I'd have a chance to do several interviews, talking with residents about their views of the country, how they thought the election process was going, and whether George Bush or Michael Dukakis would make the better president. It was fascinating for me to see Iowa's flat landscape at last, to visit a granary, and to talk with honest-to-goodness Iowa farmers.

In Miami, we focused on an apartment complex where seniors were active politically. It was an eye-opener to see just how involved they were, meeting weekly, discussing issues that were important to them in the 1988 campaign (most especially Social Security and Medicare), and how they felt about each of the candidates. They laughed and talked easily with one another and were gracious about inviting our intrusive cameras and crew into their private quarters. It was my first direct appreciation of the power of the camera, and of the effect of its presence on people's behavior: the men and women who carried this communication equipment of the twentieth century were treated with something close to awe. Much of that has changed today—people have grown accustomed to seeing cameras and TV trucks in their grocery stores and in their neighborhoods—but television cameras and radio microphones still generate a certain excitement.

Surprisingly, I found myself growing quite comfortable with television, enjoying the opportunity to do something outside the confines of a radio studio. I have always memorized fairly easily, thanks, I believe, to those early days in amateur theater. Soon, John O'Toole was giving me more and more opportunities to do interviews with leading figures on Capitol Hill. Within a short period of time, O'Toole informed me that "Modern Maturity" was planning to change format and to hire a new host and anchor for the program. He invited me to audition for the spot, which would be a coanchor position along with the writer and longtime television personality Heywood Hale Broun, who'd already been selected. So I went through a lengthy audition with Broun and was told that a decision would be made within a few weeks. The *Washington Post TV Week* got wind of the project, and reporter Patricia Brennan called to say she'd like to do an interview with me, which ran in the August 28, 1988, issue. But it wasn't just any old interview—I was right on the cover of the magazine.

The reaction was considerable, with people all over the city wondering whether I was going to leave radio for television. Callers phoned in to my program, seeking reassurance that I wouldn't abandon my daily talk show. I told them I had no intention of doing so, since it was of the utmost importance to me. And it's a good thing that was my reaction, because O'Toole ran into unexpected interference from AARP. The lobbying organization had decided it was spending too much of its resources on a program over which it had virtually no control. So, without warning and not much more than a week before production of the newly formatted program was to get under way, AARP pulled the plug. I was saddened, but grateful for the experiences I'd had. Unfortunately, it was not to be the last time I would come up against the AARP bureaucracy.

The experience with television proved useful several years later, when the producer of the now defunct CBS overnight program "Nightwatch" called to ask me whether I'd like to sit in as anchor for a few weeks. Charlie Rose, the popular host of the program for some ten years, had recently resigned, and CBS was rumored to be ready to discontinue the program, but in the interim, several substitute hosts were invited to carry on. It was a terrific experience for me, working with the professionals at CBS and getting good feedback from them, as well as from viewers and my own listeners. But it didn't last very long. CBS informed its affiliates that the show would run for only two more weeks, so I took the show off the air, offering a short commentary about what it had accomplished over its ten-year history. It was a sad moment for all of us as the set went dark for the last time.

The world of television is so very different from that of radio. Once a live radio program begins, it just goes without stopping. The mistakes, the bloopers, the misspoken words, the coughs, the pounding on the table—they're all part of the program. Television, when it's pretaped, is a vastly more time-consuming process. The other great difference is that radio fills the imagination. On radio, people have no idea what I or any of my guests look like, and therefore are more apt to concentrate on the words and their content. With television, the image becomes an intense focal point, one that can, to a degree, get in the way of what's being said and done. So while I'd have to say that I enjoyed the television experience, it was not as satisfying for me as radio.

One element of public radio and television that people often complain about is the fund-raising. Twice a year, WAMU and other local affiliates of public radio and TV around the country ask (some say beg) listeners to contribute dollars to support the broadcasts they hear and see. Having done this for more than twenty-five years, I can tell you it's a lot easier now than it used to be. In 1973, shortly after I came to WAMU, we were lucky to raise $15,000 in a full week of fund-raising. Our tactics were all wrong, but it took us years to realize that. For example, instead of carrying on with what we normally did (i.e., talk), we would play music and between selections ask listeners to contribute dollars. I remember that one year soon after I became host of the show, I was told I would be playing music by the jazz artist

Thelonious Monk for the entire two hours on the air! It wasn't a very strong enticement, not because the music wasn't fine but because it was not what listeners wanted to hear during those two hours. Beg though we did, we raised very little money. Finally, in about 1982, we realized that what listeners wanted was the talk program, so instead of bringing them a totally different kind of show, we stuck to talk and took a few minutes out of each half hour to pitch for dollars. It worked. Our one-week fund drive in the fall of 1998 brought in nearly $890,000, representing 65 percent of our operating budget for a six-month period. Quite a change from 1973.

One of the funniest fund-raising incidents occurred several years ago, when columnist and author Art Buchwald came on the program. At about twenty past the hour, Art spontaneously offered to match, dollar for dollar, every single pledge that came in from a donor in an automobile for the whole hour. I looked at him very carefully and said, "Art, are you sure you know what you're getting into?" "Of course," he said, laughing. "After all, there can't be that many folks who are going to call in and pledge from their cars." He was wrong. The phones went crazy and he could hear them ringing. One woman called in and said she was at home sick in bed but had gotten up, put on a bathrobe, and gone out to her car to call us and make a pledge, just to get Art to match it. Within ten minutes, more than $1,100 had come in from people who were driving around, listening to the program in their cars. At that point, my manager and I took pity on Art and cut off the offer. Shaking his head in disbelief, Art Buchwald wrote us a check for $1,100.

CHAPTER 23

L ITTLE BY LITTLE, I became aware that influential people were listening. The first indication came with notification that the American Association of University Women had decided to bestow an award on the program for broadcast excellence. I was excited to go to the awards ceremony and listen to the praise of the presenter. That was a huge boost for my self-esteem. The end result of the award, typically, was to motivate me to work even harder, to prove to the world that I deserved the award and that AAUW hadn't made a mistake.

Working hard meant struggling to stay on top of the news and to use all my powers of persuasion to get the finest people onto the program. By this time, my boss had finally agreed to allow me to hire a part-time producer, Ann Strainchamps, a bright and energetic young woman as interested as I am in seeking out fully qualified people for the program. She had no hesitation in calling people at the highest levels of government and making a strong pitch to them or their secretaries arguing why they should want to appear on the show. Her judgment was first-rate, and her support for me was equally important.

There were books of all kinds that came into our office, sent by New York publishers who wanted their authors to appear on talk-radio programs like mine. At first, it was just a trickle, perhaps three or four books a week. Now the traffic is overwhelming, with forty to fifty books a week competing for three to four slots. In the early days of the program, we were pleased to receive anything that looked worthwhile and might be of interest to listeners. At that time, radio was competing with television for major bookings, and television was winning; morning programs like the "Today" show won hands down. Authors and their publicists knew that an appearance on that program meant a significant boost in sales. Now the situation has changed. Readers listen to radio, and booksellers know this. NPR programs like "Morning Edition," "All Things Considered," "Fresh Air," "Public Interest," "Talk of the Nation," and "The Diane Rehm Show" have helped to alter the landscape.

One of the books that crossed my desk was a work of fiction by a world-renowned scholar from a developing country. Ann knew his work and urged me to have him on the program. I agreed, and did extensive preparation. When he arrived at the studio, he informed me that he'd never before done a live radio broadcast and was looking forward to the experience. His English was not perfect, yet it was good enough to be understood. But in the middle of the broadcast, with callers waiting on the line to ask him questions, my guest passed me a note. It said, "I have to use the toilet." Without waiting for a response or signal from me, he got up and left the studio. So there I was, forced to make up a story about his having been called away momentarily and ad-libbing long enough to allow him to get back to the microphone. In that building, unfortunately, the rest rooms were on the lower level, so it took a good five minutes for him to return, probably the longest five minutes of my on-air career. As a result of that experience, the producers who now greet guests make sure to point out the rest rooms before broadcast time.

One of the reasons for the show's growing popularity and the willingness of guests to participate was that we consistently presented a variety of views. That meant that on any given issue we would invite people from the left, right, and center of the political spectrum. The purpose of the program was not to convince people of the correctness of any single perspective, but rather to give them ideas to think about and explore further on their own. With issues such as the Israeli-Palestinian conflict, gun control, abortion, and Ronald Reagan's, George Bush's, and Bill Clinton's presidencies, we were both applauded and criticized by all sides, perceived on one day as slanting toward the ideas of the left and on another day hearing from critics that our guests were too right-wing. But no matter what the subject, the producers and I tried to maintain a fair and even-handed tone to the program.

This philosophy was severely tested in 1998, when accusations of a sexual liaison between President Clinton and Monica Lewinsky hit the front pages of the nation's newspapers. Washington was inundated with leaks, innuendos, assumptions, accusations, and denials. The talk shows, including mine, were dealing with both mainstream and tabloid press reports that could not be verified and yet were openly discussed. This wasn't easy, since we didn't want to completely exclude ourselves from the tremendous rush of events moving the capital city. Radio and television talk shows all over the country were concentrating on Monica all the time. We were, however, dealing with a majority of listeners who were becoming ever more angry with us each time we broadcast a program dealing with, first, the accusations, then the impeachment, and finally, the trial. I received phone calls, e-mails, and letters arguing that there were other, more vital issues being ignored because of the Clinton scandal and congressional concentration on the subject, so we decided to confine our discussions of each week's developments to the "Friday News Roundup," our most-listened-to hour of the week. Even these weekly discussions, which involved reporters and commentators both critical and supportive of the president, and which also focused on other national and international news, seemed to infuriate listeners, who continued to accuse the media of having played a large role in creating a national noncrisis.

Despite the fact that polls showed a majority turned off by the scandal and debate, an estimated seventy million viewers watched as Monica Lewinsky was interviewed by ABC's Barbara Walters. Next came Lewinsky's best-selling book, with more details about her relationship with the president, closely followed by another successful tell-all book, this one written by George Stephanopolous, about his years with Bill Clinton. If there are real lessons here about public distaste for scandalous stories and media behavior, it may be too early to learn them. But the Clinton crisis fit in with the evolution of talk radio as I have watched it unfold over the past twenty-five years. In 1973, talk radio seemed a quiet place for hosts, guests, and callers to express their feelings. It was almost an extension of the back fence, where friends, neighbors, and strangers alike could share their thoughts and ideas without fear of arousing hostility. Of course there were differences of opinion, sometimes extreme. But the relationships could be counted on, and the remarks were tempered by the realization that those differences disappeared in the face of common interests, such as families, children, schools, and the concerns of the country as a whole.

During the past quarter century, however, there's been a major shift, and I do believe talk radio has been a significant force behind that change. Without benefit of editors, factcheckers, or tempering voices, talk radio has played a central part in changing and reshaping the dynamic of the national conversation. It has moved from a role of reflecting the news to that of making the news. To my mind, the changes began to take hold in the late 1980s, when the talk increasingly turned to politics and, as it did so, talk radio began to gain national prominence.

In early 1989, a talk-show host in Seattle, Mike Siegel, professing outrage over a congressional pay raise, urged his listeners to send tea bags to Capitol Hill (recalling, of course, the Boston Tea Party) as a protest. Some forty to fifty other broadcasters joined with Siegel, and together they created a national uproar. Thousands of listeners protested the raise by writing, phoning, and faxing their representatives, and swamping congressional switchboards. The radio talk-show lines lit up as well, and the talk hosts received national attention on network news programs. Ultimately, members of Congress voted to defeat the pay raise. Talk radio had moved onto the national political scene. At the time, I wrote an op-ed piece for the *Washington Post* saying that I thought talk-show hosts should shun taking positions on political subjects. For one thing, I believed, and still believe, that because we have daily access to people in their homes, offices, and cars, we have an important responsibility to be even-handed in our approach to subjects rather than to try to use our microphones to influence people's thinking. As a result of that essay, I was asked to appear on the "Today" show in a debate with Jerry Williams, a talk-show host in Boston who'd long enjoyed his status as a broadcast agitator. Jane Pauley was the host at the time, and I must say I thoroughly enjoyed myself. My thrust, with a smile on my face, was that many of the talk-show hosts around the country, including Mr. Williams, were looking for higher ratings and more advertising money by being as outrageous as possible. I argued that none of us had been elected by the citizens of this country, and that, within the context of a free and open society, we had a responsibility to conduct programs representing all sides of the debate. I said that too many talk-show hosts were promoting their own personal political agenda by including on their programs only callers who reflected that perspective.

Mr. Williams said that was ridiculous, and began to attack me as merely a public broadcaster, one who was supported by government money and didn't have to worry about ratings. His tone was sneering and condescending. And then Jane Pauley decided to take a call from one of Mr. Williams's listeners in the Boston area. It was not a good moment for Jerry Williams because the caller echoed my sentiments, not only about talk radio in general but about Mr. Williams in particular and his practice of screening callers to include only those sympathetic to his point of view. Jerry Williams got red in the face, began to sputter and spout, at which point Jane Pauley said we were out of time. Actually, I was told afterward that it was one of the longest segments the "Today" program had ever run, lasting some eight or nine minutes. Several years later, I spoke with a television consultant who coaches people who are learning to use the medium effectively. He told me that he uses that nine-minute segment as a training device, pointing to how successful I had been in reaching the audience, and to Jerry Williams's performance as a prime example of what not to do in a television interview. Unfortunately, none of the talk shows around the country, the vast majority of which were hosted by men, paid the slightest bit of attention to what I said. In fact, I went on to debate many more of these hosts, including Rush Limbaugh in the early days of his career.

After their early success, several of the talk hosts debated whether to pool their collective vocal resources. The idea was to choose other issues on which they might come together and repeat the pay-raise effort. But it soon became clear that with egos as large as theirs, there was no way they could agree about much of anything. They did, however, create a national organization that holds yearly gatherings and promotes the overall interests of talk radio. I've chosen not to join, since most of their members are commercial as opposed to public broadcasters. The approach to subjects and guests of public broadcasting's talk shows is for the most part very different from that of commercial radio. At times, as I've listened to talk shows on some commercial stations, I've wondered why guests agree to appear, when the purpose seems to be to humiliate them and engage them in rancorous and even ugly debate. On the other hand, there are hosts like Don Imus who do take up serious issues and have first-rate conversations with guests.

During these twenty-five years in talk radio, I've seen it change from being a medium few people listened to or talked about into an important force in shaping public opinion. From a relatively small base of listeners in the late seventies, these programs have grown in both number and reach. There are now some five thousand talk shows around the country, reaching millions of people. Rush Limbaugh alone claims an audience of twenty million. Many, like Rush, focus exclusively on politics, but now there are as many varieties of talk shows as there are preferences. There are personal psychology shows, with Dr. Laura Schlessinger leading the pack. One of the most successful programs on public radio is "Car Talk," an automobile repair show. There are travel shows, gardening shows, dating shows—you name it, it's out there, both on commercial and public radio. Part of the growth is due to the introduction of FM radios into cars, as well as the move of radios into the workplace. When I was growing up in Washington, there were very few employers who allowed workers to bring radios into their offices or shops. Now radios are on in most places of business, from law offices to government cubicles.

When my own program began, in 1979, there were just a few thousand listeners in the Washington area, and most were women in the home. The latest figures indicate that we have more than seven hundred thousand listeners around the country, with an equal number of men and women listening. Some 40 percent are in their offices, another 40 percent listen in their cars, and the rest work in their homes. And the telephone lines are busy from the moment we open the show.

Participating in the growth of this program has been enormously exciting for me. In the beginning, as I've said, people barely knew what public radio was, much less "The Diane Rehm Show," but little by little, the change began to occur. Whereas initially an invitation to appear on the program would be met with something like "What did you say the name of the show was?" gradually the recognition grew. Reaching the appropriate people for a given subject began to be easier, and the number of refusals began to decline. The reputation of the program as a good vehicle for solid discussion around important issues was spreading.

During the evolutionary period of talk radio, I watched changes take place in the audience itself. People now rely on talk radio to inform them. They hear opinions expressed, and when they form their own, many times they're based on what they hear. People of influence listen and participate. For many years, people complained that only the wealthy and powerful had the ear of Congress, the White House, the judiciary, or leaders of industry. Talk radio has, to a certain extent, changed that, demonstrating its ability to provide access, and the power to get action. Callers have come to relish the impact they can have on public discourse. And now prominent public figures, including the president himself, authors, entertainers, and journalists, all recognize the value of direct two-way contact with the ordinary people whose lives they affect.

I have frequently been surprised when, in the midst of a discussion on a policy issue, a member of the administration or a member of Congress has called in to make a comment. They all realize the value of making their points heard. Recently we did a program on Medicare, a subject about which there has been much talk and even more controversy. California congressman Pete Stark, the ranking Democrat on the House health care subcommittee, called to ensure that his perspective would be part of the program. But as talk radio has grown in numbers and influence, so, too, has my concern about its impact on the dialogue in this country. In a sense, the very anonymity that callers enjoy has, to a certain extent, contributed to a hostile atmosphere on the airwaves.

Several months ago, Kathleen Hall Jamieson, dean of the Annenberg School of Communication, came on the program to talk about her book on the media's role in the political process. A caller phoned in with some choice comments about his least favorite politician. Dr. Jamieson responded that the fact that a caller feels free to make such comments from the privacy and anonymity of his or her own home fuels that kind of hostility. If you were face-to-face with someone with whom you disagreed, you would probably be more inclined to temper your language, but when there are no perceived consequences to what you say, you feel as though you have a free ride. It's only through the efforts of a host that that kind of language and behavior can be tempered. If a host is also engaging in outrageous rhetoric, it's likely to be reflected in the tone of the caller.

There's another factor that's spurred the growth of talk radio, and that's the emergence of the angry citizen. Whether the focus is a Supreme Court nominee like Robert Bork in 1987 or Clarence Thomas in 1991, Hillary Clinton's activities on behalf of health care reform in 1993, the Republicans' Contract with America in 1995, or Bill Clinton's relationship with women, talk radio has created a forum for those who wish to air their views, no matter how extreme or outrageous, for public consumption. Callers have grown sophisticated in their use of the airways to promote their own ideas or biases. Instead of asking questions, many callers make statements. Rather than seek information, they challenge experts. Lobbyists for environmental causes, gun ownership, or abortion rights call in knowing that their arguments, once aired, will become part of the public debate. The toll-free lines are open to all who want to participate. The air-waves become pathways for the spread of information, opinion, or rumor, accurate or otherwise. What sometimes results is an unspoken partnership between hosts seeking higher ratings and individuals seeking to use talk radio to further their own causes.

Truth can be a casualty. One example in particular stands out in my mind. After the suicide of White House aide Vincent Foster in June 1993, talk radio was filled with stories of murder in a Washington apartment, the transport of Mr. Foster's body to Fort Marcy Park in Virginia, and a cover-up by park police. Even today, despite a statement from special Whitewater counsel Kenneth Starr confirming that Mr. Foster's death was indeed a suicide, the rumors continue. But in the immediate aftermath of his death, the outpouring of speculation was rampant. I remember one day when I had an hour of open phones during which people could call in to talk about any subject. A man identifying himself as Bob called to say he had a theory about Vince Foster. When I asked him whether it was simply a theory with no facts to back it up, he yelled into the phone that though it was only a theory, he had a "right" to state it on talk radio. I said to him very quietly, "Not on my program you don't." And I cut him off. I received both support and criticism for that action, but it seemed to me at the time, and seems even more so now, that talk radio should not be used as a vehicle to spread rumors. That, however, is precisely how it's often being used these days.

I remember an earlier time in my career when I was less pre-pared for a comparable incident. A caller phoned in with news that had far-reaching implications. In early May 1989, then House Speaker Jim Wright was faced with accusations that he had violated House rules and committed improprieties in connection with the publication of his memoirs. In the midst of that controversy, the *Washington Post* ran a Style section piece about his top legislative aide, John Mack, the gist being that, as a young man, he'd been accused of savagely beating and stabbing a young woman named Pamela Small, leaving her for dead. He had served two years in prison for the offense. As soon as the piece was published, Speaker Wright and many of his colleagues on the Hill jumped to Mack's defense. The *Washington Post* reported that "Wright had hired Mack, an ex-felon, out of prison, in 1975. The job the Speaker gave him was influential in the decision to allow him to leave jail after serving twenty-seven months of a fifteen-year (with seven years suspended) sentence. At the time of the incident, John Mack's brother was married to Speaker Wright's daughter."

Many members of Congress joined Wright in praising Mack as a valued staffer and a solid family man who had made a single youthful mistake. They stood as a chorus, commending Mack as having completely straightened out his life. Many spoke of him as an invaluable employee of the Congress. It was even suggested by some members that the incident was not as serious as had been portrayed in the *Post*, raising questions about the reputation and veracity of the young woman involved. The matter might have died there were it not for talk radio. This time, my program played a central role. On the day the *Washington Post* published the article, I opened the phones and callers wanted to talk about the actions of the Speaker, as well as those of his aide. At three minutes before noon, just as I was about to sign off, I took one last call from a man who spoke rapidly and angrily. He said that John Mack was not the reformed innocent his defenders made him out to be. In fact, he shouted, John Mack had raped his wife, a teenage classmate of Mack's, two years before he attacked Pamela Small. When I heard his words, I said, "Those are pretty serious charges you're making, sir." He said all of his charges could be verified by the Fairfax County, Virginia, Police Department. By this point, the clock had reached noon and it was time to sign off, so I asked the caller to call me back on my office phone so that I could speak with him further. He promised he would.

I emerged from the studio stunned, and realized that all the switchboard lines were ringing. Apparently every news organization in Washington had heard the caller and wanted to find out more about his allegations. By the time the caller (whose name was John) phoned me again, I had already taken calls from the Associated Press (AP), the *New York Times*, and United Press International (UPI). I explained that, so far, I knew nothing more than what the caller had said on the air, and that I hadn't had an opportunity to follow up on his claims.

I spent about a half hour on the phone with John, listening to his allegations and asking questions about how I might verify the story. He reiterated that I could check with Fairfax County Police, but said his wife would not talk with me. He did, however, suggest that his wife's mother might be willing to have a phone conversation with me, and he gave me her number. I phoned John's mother-in-law, who did, in fact, confirm his story that her daughter had been raped by John Mack, and that the event had been so traumatic that she would not talk about it with anyone. I then tracked down a knowledgeable officer at Fairfax County Police Headquarters, who confirmed that a record of a prior charge against John Mack did exist, but he refused to go into details with me over the phone.

Between noon and four-thirty that afternoon, I fielded over ninety calls, primarily from news organizations who'd seen a report of the caller's allegations on the AP wire. I was still no further along in verifying the story, however, since the young woman involved would not talk with me. But despite her reluctance, the damage had been done. The next day, accounts of the call appeared in all the major newspapers, and then television news got into the act. Talk shows around the country were also buzzing with the allegation. The uproar reached a fever pitch late that afternoon when John Mack resigned, saying how much he appreciated Speaker Wright and the House of Representatives for giving him "a second chance," but that he had no alternative but to go.

It was, for me, proof of the extraordinary power of the media, most especially those outlets that operate without a hierarchy of editors and fact-checkers. I've often looked back on that moment when "John" called in, and thought that had I been a newspaper reporter sitting at a desk and taking his allegations down on a pad of paper, the story might have had a very different outcome. Though I might eventually have been able to verify his statements, they would have had to run the gamut of fact-checkers and editors. It would have taken longer, and it might not have had the same impact as it had when it was heard on the air by many thousands of listeners throughout the Washington metropolitan area who had just read about Mack in that morning's *Washington Post*. Finally, "John" was so passionate, articulate, and persuasive that listeners had a firsthand opportunity to make up their minds without the mediating influence of reporters and columnists "shaping" the story. I was absolutely amazed by the impact that a single phone call, from an unidentified source, could have on a man's career and life. If ever I needed a reminder of the responsibility that people in my line of work have, this was surely a good one.

Part Three

LOSING—
AND FINDING—
MY VOICE

CHAPTER 24

BOUT EIGHT YEARS AGO, I began to experi-
ence voice problems. It has been a long ordeal, but perhaps it speaks to the intensity of pressure that some (or
all) of us, whether female or male, feel even as we achieve a measure of success in our chosen professions.

It started with Advil, shortly after it became a nonprescription,
over-the-counter drug. I began to use it as a substitute for aspirin
or Bufferin, for headaches, muscle aches, sore throats, or sleepless-
ness. Whenever one of those symptoms appeared, I popped two
Advil, perhaps as many as two or three times a week. Usually, one
dose seemed enough to take care of the problem. Within several
months of fairly regular usage, I developed a shallow cough. At
first, I didn't pay much attention to it, but little by little it began
to interfere with my ability to speak on the air. In other words, in
the middle of a sentence I would cough. Not for long, mind you,
and not with any depth. Just long enough to interrupt what I was

saying, or in the middle of a guest's comments. After talking with my doctor and being checked out by both an ear, nose, and throat doctor and a pulmonary specialist, none of whom could come up with any answers, I tried cough syrups and various medications, all to no avail. Finally, after an examination that involved putting a tube down into my throat turned up nothing, I came home frustrated and in tears. Because the examination had left my throat feeling sore and raw, I reached for the Advil. It was at that instant, and for the first time, that I read the patient package insert. And lo and behold, it said, "This medication may produce asthma-like symptoms." The patient package insert has since been changed to warn "aspirin sensitive patients . . . [not to take Advil if they] have had a severe allergic reaction to aspirin, e.g.—asthma, swelling, shock or hives." Up to that time, however, I had never had a problem with aspirin or Bufferin. After all the examinations and consultations, the diagnosis came down to overuse of an over-the-counter drug. The experience taught me a good lesson: don't overlook what can seem to be the most innocuous causes of medical problems.

Unfortunately, however, the voice problems didn't stop there, and I became increasingly worried. Every cold or sore throat seemed to end up settling in my vocal cords (I've since learned they're not "cords" at all, but rather "folds"), leaving me without a voice for days, followed by a raspy hoarseness. Three or four times a year, usually when I was at my most exhausted, the cold and sore throat would set in. I was in therapy at the time, continuing to deal with problems of low self-esteem and a lack of belief in myself. I can remember my therapist, Jack Harris, suggesting that my frequent sore throats and loss of voice were a way my body was telling me to ease up, to let go of some of the tensions surrounding both my professional and personal life. Eventually, with the help of vitamin C, regular flu shots, exercise, good diet, and lots of weekend rest, I was able to put the era of periodic colds and sore throats behind me. But I couldn't seem to rid myself completely of the vocal difficulties.

In 1992, a media specialist for AARP approached me about the possibility of doing a weekly, hour-long radio program for them. The program would focus on news and feature stories pertaining to the elderly, everything from changes in Social Security and Medicare payments to scams against the elderly and automobile accident rates. The intention was to offer the program to public radio stations across the country. The understanding was that the staff of AARP would do the groundwork and consult with me about guest selection and program content, while I would host each interview. It was also understood that there would be no effort on the part of AARP's executives to influence the editorial content of the program. In other words, we would be free to carry on an honest discussion, bringing all points of view to the table, even on issues where AARP might disagree with some of the opinions being expressed.

For about a year, that agreement worked just fine. Public Radio International (PRI) picked us up because I was hosting the show, and before long we were being distributed to fifty stations. The guests during that first year included Health and Human Services Secretary Donna Shalala and Attorney General Janet Reno. Dr. Shalala is Lebanese, and very warm and engaging, so we had a great time together. But I remember feeling concerned about the attorney general. She was not an easy talker, and seemed to have great difficulty looking me in the eye, which was particularly odd since she was sitting less than two feet away from me, across a tiny table in an extremely small and cramped studio. The conversation was stressful enough to begin with because she seemed so uncomfortable, but when we got around to opening the phones for listeners' calls, things got even worse. She had difficulty responding to specific questions, in part, I think, because she was so unaccustomed to an open exchange with the public. She began picking at the skin around her nails, tearing off bits and pieces until her fingers began to show blood. I stared in horrified fascination as this self-inflicted wounding continued, and was tempted to put my hand over hers and say, "It's all right. It's really all right." But, of course, I did nothing of the sort. It was relatively early in her tenure as attorney general, and I'm sure she wanted to be ultracautious in her comments. I think of that hour I spent with her each time I see her on television.

By the second year of the broadcast, problems began to surface. There was some negative feedback from AARP executives about topics we had chosen, like supplemental health insurance for the elderly and driving examinations for those over the age of seventy, plus pressure to include more AARP spokespersons on the air. For me, the issue was a clear one. From the start, I had been assured that the producer and I would have complete control over the program and that there would be no interference from the organization. This had been a crucial factor in my signing on with the show, since I felt that the freedom of operation, independence of thought, and professional standing I had maintained for so many years could be compromised if the program, and I as its host, were considered simply a "mouthpiece" for the largest lobbying organization in the United States. So I began to balk, both at the choice of certain subjects and at the selection of certain guests.

It was in the middle of this period of tension that, during a recording session just before the program was to air one day, my voice quivered slightly. The producer of the program remarked on it, saying, "Is something wrong? Are you nervous?" I quickly waved off his comment and rerecorded the few lines. Clearly, something had happened, but I had no idea that within four years that small problem would become the greatest challenge of my professional life.

Not long after that incident, I was informed that AARP was not going to renew my contract for a third year. This came without any warning whatsoever. I was particularly annoyed since just the previous month I'd been asked by the organization to fly to Los Angeles to do a series of interviews, a trip I'd agreed to even though it meant taking time off from my own program on

WAMU. During our time in L.A., there was absolutely no indication that a change of hosts was in the offing, and certainly no
sign that my work was deficient in any way. When the ax fell,
I remember feeling not only angry but used. Of course, any
employer is entitled to terminate an employee if that employee is
not performing satisfactorily, but I felt that the action had been
carried out in a less than open and honest manner. My professional
ego was definitely deflated, and contributed to my anger. I hated
being "let go," and though one part of me felt I had failed, I knew I
had stood up for my own beliefs and held to my standards.

More importantly, that voice tremor had really begun to
worry me. I started listening for it, wondering when it might
appear next. Sure enough, it did manifest itself occasionally, but
not so often that anyone else seemed to notice it or, at least, remark on it. Whenever I heard it, I tried to quickly move past it,
thinking that getting on to the next word would help fool both
me and my listeners into believing it had never happened. But
slowly, gradually, I began to hear the tremor more frequently.

I finally got up the nerve to consult a throat specialist at
Georgetown University. After doing a thorough physical examination and finding nothing out of the ordinary, he referred me
to a speech pathologist, Dr. Susan Miller, also at Georgetown.
Together, we began to work on breath support. Apparently, during all the years I'd been broadcasting, I'd never learned to breathe
correctly. In other words, I was taking breaths not by expanding
my diaphragm, as singers are taught to do, but more shallowly,
from my upper chest. Consequently, she said, I was running out of
breath at the end of each sentence, forcing a strain in my vocal
folds. She urged me to breathe more frequently within sentences,
avoiding a long-standing habit of putting too many words into one
breath. In addition, she noted a muscular tension in my jaw and
tongue, a situation that also made it difficult to speak with ease.

Dr. Miller is a wonderful coach and an extraordinarily supportive person. Nonetheless, I believed that what was happening

to me could not simply be attributed to improper breathing techniques or muscle tension. So even as she assigned me exercises to help strengthen my entire respiratory apparatus, deep in my heart I believed there was a physical, perhaps organic, reason for my difficulties. In fact, there were "homework assignments" I simply could not perform because I had so little control over my voice.

After several months at Georgetown and with John's encouragement, I made an appointment to see a physician in Philadelphia, Dr. Robert Sataloff, who had an entire clinic devoted to voice problems. John and I took an early train for a 10:00 a.m. appointment. As we walked into the clinic, we were astounded to see fifty or sixty people waiting. At four o'clock that afternoon, after we'd been encouraged to walk around the city and have lunch and then return, we saw Dr. Sataloff and about six of his assistants. We talked about my problem very briefly, and then he anesthetized my throat (a hideous experience that leaves you thinking you can't swallow, creating absolute panic; fortunately, the effects don't last long). Inserting a long, thin tube with a light and a tiny camera down into my throat, he examined my vocal folds and confirmed that there were no physical obstructions or nodules creating the problem. He did note a slight tremor on one side of the vocal fold but suggested that it was very minor. His diagnosis: acid reflux, a fairly common ailment in which the muscle at the base of the esophagus weakens, allowing small amounts of the acid used to break down food to seep up into the back of the throat. Typical symptoms are heartburn and hoarseness, both of which I had been prone to. (President Clinton has also been diagnosed with this problem, leading to repeated bouts of hoarseness, both during his campaigns and throughout his presidency.)

The medication Dr. Sataloff prescribed was Prilosec, a drug that neutralizes or reduces the amount of acid in the stomach. Nevertheless, he wanted me to see a neurologist at the Jefferson Medical College in Philadelphia to rule out any possible neurological disorder. And so, several weeks later, John and I went back to Philadelphia to see Dr. Steven Mandel, clinical professor of neurology and a specialist in neuromuscular diseases. He first had me undergo testing by magnetic resonance imaging (MRI) and then brought me to his office for an extensive neurological examination. Dr. Mandel found virtually no tremulousness in my voice; he noticed a very slight palatal tremor but no evidence of tongue tremor. His recommendation was to continue taking the drug Prilosec and to introduce small doses of Inderal, a beta-blocker used to lower blood pressure. It's sometimes used by performers before going onstage to reduce stage fright, or even by surgeons before they operate to steady their hands. I used it for a time, as prescribed. It seemed to help at first, but after a brief period it proved useless. My voice was as unreliable as ever, and its tremor was back in evidence.

In the midst of the growing anxiety about my voice, a long-awaited opportunity arose. The manager of WAMU-FM, Kim Hodgson, after years of campaigning and bargaining on my part, said he would entertain the idea of airing my program nationally if I could raise the money. In other words, the station itself didn't have the resources to underwrite national distribution, but if the money were available, the timing seemed right. Public stations around the country were beginning to move away from classical music and jazz programming toward news and talk, and they were looking for quality programs to meet their needs. Given the low-budget world of public broadcasting, however, those stations couldn't pay for such a program; initially, it would have to be provided free of charge. At the time, the only nationally broadcast live call-in show available to noncommercial stations was coming from National Public Radio, a program called "Talk of the Nation." I felt that listeners around the country would respond to "The Diane Rehm Show" with the same enthusiasm demonstrated by our audience in the Washington metropolitan area, so without hesitation, though I'd never previously raised money for any cause, I said I would do it.

The estimate for the first year, including the cost of satellite transmission, hiring a person to market the program to other NPR stations, and a toll-free number for calls from listeners around the country, was $120,000. In fact, the amount raised had to be double that, since no station would agree to air the program if it were guaranteed for only one year. To those in the television broadcast business, $240,000 would seem a paltry sum, but radio is much less expensive to produce. Even so, no matter how formidable the amount seemed to be, I was certain I could raise it.

I went first to June Hechinger. She and her husband, John, had on several occasions expressed their appreciation for the program and their amazement that it wasn't broadcast nationally. They have both been enormously generous to many causes in both the civic and the artistic world, but when we were seated at lunch, my heart was in my throat. Then, in her simple and straightforward way, she said, "What do you need?" Since I didn't know her very well, I was surprised and pleased at her directness. I then expressed my belief in the program and its value, my conviction that other stations across the country would welcome the show, and my feeling that public radio would present to its listeners an alternative to the Rush Limbaughs and G. Gordon Liddys of the world. We could offer real conversations, with government officials, politicians, artists, musicians, writers, and teachers. We could bring informed and reasoned discussion to the air and invite people who were genuinely interested in expanding their understanding to call us from around the country. Without a moment's hesitation, June agreed to be my first contributor, and the project was at last off the ground.

If you've ever been involved in a fund-raising project, you know how overwhelming it can be. The thought of asking individuals I didn't know very well for money in substantial amounts seemed awfully pushy to me, but that first success gave me courage, so I next turned to Knight Kiplinger, another longtime fan of the program, who came to the station for a late-afternoon discussion. Kim Hodgson and I both talked about the program, the caliber of guests we were able to attract, the growth of listenership over the years, and the service to the community. When we got to the idea of national broadcast, he asked some probing questions about how widely accepted the broadcast might be by individual public stations. Kim told him that though we couldn't guarantee any particular number, several stations had already expressed interest in moving to a news/talk format and would likely be good prospects. At the end of the meeting, Knight indicated interest but said he would have to talk with others regarding any specific amount of money his corporation might be willing to give. He was most encouraging, however, and promised to get back to us in a couple of days. And he did, with a very generous contribution that gave me hope we would reach our goal more quickly than I had imagined.

One day during that period of fund-raising, the writer Margaret Atwood came to my studio for perhaps the third or fourth time. Ever since *The Handmaid's Tale* was published, I've been one of her loyal fans. *Cat's Eye* and *The Robber Bride* are also favorites. She and I had had some fascinating conversations during her various publicity tours, and she was always complimentary about the interviews and the caliber of our callers, saying she thought they were the best in the country. Before our interview began, I mentioned to her that we hoped eventually to take the show national but were still in the process of raising the necessary funds. She immediately asked whether I had talked with her editor at Doubleday, Nan Talese. When I said I hadn't, she told me she was planning to have breakfast with Nan the next day and would mention the project to her. The very next afternoon, I received a phone call from an interested Nan Talese. I sent her material, outlining the projected costs and benefits, and three weeks later we received the news that Nan Talese and Doubleday were on board.

Several weeks later, CNN host Larry King came in for an

interview. Larry and I have known each other for years and have supported each other along the way. When I told him about the fund-raising effort, Larry said, "You've come to the right person. I'll not only make a contribution myself, but I'll get a substantial amount of additional money for you." And so he did, presenting our case to the Milken Foundation and shepherding the request through the bureaucratic maze that is part of any large charitable institution. Several months later, we received a very generous check from the foundation and another check from Larry himself. But it wasn't just the large contributions that helped us make our target. It was the support of many, many individuals, both personal friends and friends of friends who decided to make a direct donation. I was immensely pleased when, in only seven months, we reached our goal.

What followed, in May 1995, was the successful launch of national distribution of "The Diane Rehm Show." Even before the first satellite transmission, we had four stations on board. Kim Hodgson told me that if we had ten stations by the end of 1995, he would consider the operation a success. Instead, much to our surprise and delight, we ended up with twenty.

One of our first guests after we began broadcasting nationally was Hillary Rodham Clinton. (I had heard that she was a regular listener to the program and had made favorable comments about it. In fact, the president had been photographed by the Associated Press with a WAMU coffee mug in his hand, a premium sent to the White House after the Clintons made their first contribution during one of our fund drives.) The entire building on Brandywine Street was in a state of frenzy in anticipation of her arrival. The Secret Service arrived the day before to check out every corner of the building, and their dogs had been brought in to double-check. She arrived, as had been requested, fifteen minutes before the broadcast, and was taken to a small private studio to make a few phone calls and relax. When I came out to meet her, I was immediately impressed with her grace and beauty. I don't think television cameras or still photos accurately reflect just how pretty a woman she is. Beyond that, however, is her warmth, which comes through genuinely and directly. As for me, I was very nervous, but her manner helped to calm me down.

Mrs. Clinton was interested in the computer I had in front of me and asked questions about how the calls came into the studio. Then she saw me insert a tiny earpiece, which I've used for years instead of those huge headphones most radio broadcasters wear, a pair of which lay in front of her on the table. She picked up the headphones and realized that they would really mess up her beautifully coiffed hairdo. I offered her instead an earpiece similar to mine, which she gratefully accepted, and then we laughingly began to talk about our "hair" problem. She commented on how the press liked to focus on how she wore her hair and the many times she changed her hairdo, and confided that this was the one part of her daily life she could have complete control over and so took great pleasure in making those changes. Mrs. Clinton seemed completely relaxed and never asked what questions might be in store for her, knowing that listeners would be calling in and that we would not be screening the callers. During the hour, we talked about her failed efforts to achieve health care reform, and the extent to which she believed the public had turned against the idea because of "attack" ads generated by Republicans and the health care industry opposed to her and her husband. She spoke about the strong negative reactions some men and women have toward females who take positions of leadership. On a more personal note, she spoke about how she and the president had worked so hard to give their daughter, Chelsea, a normal life in a very public environment.

When we opened the phones, the callers were polite but pointed in their questions, asking why the president had given her such a prominent leadership role in health care reform, and whether there might have been a greater chance for success had she not been involved. One caller suggested that members of Congress felt they could not pose the tough questions to her that they might have had someone else been coordinating the effort. I asked whether she felt she had made a mistake in holding some of the planning meetings in secret and thereby generating even more hostility. She acknowledged that some mistakes might have been made but said she believed that the basic ideas of the health care reform plan were sound. She felt that because the health care industry was so opposed to change, the effort would have met with defeat no matter who had led it.

At the end of the 10:00 to 11:00 a.m. hour, Mrs. Clinton said she would be delighted to stay for yet another half hour in order to take more calls from listeners. I was amazed because I knew her aides were anxious for her to move on, but her decision was just one example of her graciousness throughout the morning. She answered each question articulately and forthrightly, never once referring to a written notation or pausing for a statistic. She knew what she wanted to say in response to each question posed to her and spoke with ease. Her answers never sounded rehearsed. At the same time, she was attentive, listening carefully and thanking listeners warmly. At the end of the ninety minutes, Mrs. Clinton took the time to shake hands with each of the forty or so people on WAMU's staff and then posed for pictures. For all of us, it was a heady morning.

During the initial period of national distribution of "The Diane Rehm Show," WAMU had undertaken satellite transmission of the program independently, without financial support from National Public Radio. But when NPR saw the total carrying strength of the show, they announced that they would begin to offer stations across the country a "Talk Track," to consist of six hours of talk programming beginning at 10:00 a.m. Eastern time with my two-hour show, followed by one hour of "Fresh Air," one hour of "The Derek McGinty Show" (now "Public Interest"), followed by "Talk of the Nation." When then NPR vice president for news, Bill Buzenberg, made the announcement at a Public Radio conference in Washington, he said that

NPR had wanted to initiate this project for quite a while but had postponed it, believing the time was not yet right. But then, he said, "a funny thing happened. Diane Rehm went national, and when we saw the successful carriage her show generated, we decided the time was right." I was sitting in the front row of the auditorium that day, and I was bursting with pride.

By January 1996, the NPR "Talk Track" was launched with great fanfare and much publicity. Even stations who'd had doubts about shifting from music formats to talk reported great acceptance from their listeners. And when the first round of on-air fund-raisers came, the contributions were up rather than down. It gave me great satisfaction to see the idea I'd worked on for so many years supported by so many others in the NPR system. Before long, stations that carried my program were inviting me to come and speak to their listeners. Within the course of several months, I went to San Diego and Chicago to broadcast from the Republican and Democratic national conventions, to Dallas, Indianapolis, St. Louis, and Cleveland to give speeches and attend station fund-raisers. Here in Washington, the launch of national broadcast increased the number of requests from individuals and organizations inviting me to speak or to participate in or lead panel discussions. My views were sought on political topics as well as on the media. Since my approach to talk radio was decidedly different from that of many others in the medium, I was frequently asked to debate talk hosts who had no qualms about bashing politicians or taking a hard-line stance on any issue they felt was newsworthy. Social invitations became more frequent as well, many to events I felt obliged to attend; others were occasions for pure enjoyment with friends and acquaintances here in Washington. All the attention and excitement made me pause, however, wondering why I still felt like "a little Arab girl" who really didn't belong.

CHAPTER 25

*T*HE PACE BEGAN to accelerate. For years, I'd been rising at 5:00 a.m. to exercise on a Nordic Track. Then, without eating breakfast (since I feared that some foods or liquids might somehow be contributing to my ongoing voice problems), I'd go into the office at about 7:30 or 8:00 a.m., read the newspapers, and check for any changes that needed to be made to the scripts for the day. I'd stay at the office until six or six-thirty in the evening, reading for upcoming programs, taking phone calls, or responding to mail. And I would set aside time late in the afternoon to work on my memoir. I'd finally reach home about seven in the evening, utterly exhausted, have dinner at about eight, and go off to bed at around ten.

This was an extraordinarily difficult period, not only for me but for John. My voice was now a constant worry. I was both depressed and extremely anxious. Each night at the dinner table, I would tell him I had serious doubts as to whether I could go on.

By January 1998, the problem had reached a point where I couldn't count on being able to get my words out. Instead of concentrating on the conversation between my guests and me, I was worried that my voice might desert me. Then, hearing my voice when words finally did emerge, I was embarrassed, because it sounded as though someone were strangling me. I felt devastated. I cried again and again, wondering how I could find the courage to resign, to give up a job I loved so much. John was supportive and understanding, but it seemed to both of us at the time that we'd done everything we could possibly have done to discover the cause of this miserable affliction.

To compound the problem, I wasn't sleeping well. Since the Advil experience, I was reluctant to use any kind of sedative. Usually, I'd fall asleep promptly at 10:00 p.m. unless we were out for an event or dinner and then awaken at 2:00 or 3:00 a.m. I'd turn on a light and read, hoping that within half an hour or so my eyelids would droop and I'd fall back to sleep, but that began happening less and less frequently. I'd then force myself to get up at five, hoping that the exercise would help to perk me up despite the lack of sleep.

During those sleepless nights, I couldn't stop worrying about whether my voice would hold up for another day of broadcasting, and whether the doctors and I were missing something. I'd think back to that morning's broadcast, remembering in excruciating detail the instants when the tremor could be heard or a crack appeared in my voice. I'd even torture myself by listening to portions of the evening rebroadcast of the program. Finally, I had to stop doing that, knowing I was adding to my distress. I'd toss and turn, unable to put aside the fear that my career in radio was coming to an end just as I was beginning to reap the rewards of my long effort to create a program of value heard nationally.

Not surprisingly, my voice was the first thing I thought about as I got up in the morning. I thought about it with every sip of water I took, with every word of greeting I spoke to John. I was constantly testing, evaluating, judging just how I might sound on the air that day. I did the vocal exercises prescribed by Dr. Miller in front of the mirror as I fixed my hair and applied my makeup, and while driving to the office. And as soon as I got to the studio, the worry would escalate. Each morning, I'd question whether I could manage to get through the prerecording necessary before the live program began at 10:00 a.m. I encountered some of my greatest difficulty when reading introductory scripts into the microphone. My engineers were kind and patient, never once showing irritation if I had to rerecord because the tremor and the strain were so prominent, but the prerecording sessions took longer and longer to complete. What should have taken no more than five to ten minutes was now taking up to twenty to thirty minutes, just to have it sound barely acceptable. Then, when the program went on the air, live, at 10:07 a.m., I'd say "Good morning" to my guests with as much strength as I could muster, trying to start the conversation with as brief a question as possible so as to deflect the talk away from me. Anticipating the show each morning was agony.

In mid-February, Kim Hodgson came into my office to ask about my health and express concern about my voice. This was the first time he'd broached the subject. He said he had heard from several people in the NPR system who had also commented on what he termed an increasing "tightness" in the throat. I remember getting up and closing the door to my office so that we could talk privately. I then began to relate to him the long saga of my efforts to find out why I was having these problems, the various specialists I'd seen, and the tests I'd undergone. He listened sympathetically and made some suggestions, such as finding ways to relax, perhaps through meditation or yoga. But deep inside, I continued to reject the notion that the problem was simply anxiety. I was certain that there was something physical creating the problem, and that if I searched hard enough, I would find it, just as I had earlier discovered the problem with Advil.

Kim's visit was the ultimate wake-up call I needed. Now it was clear I wasn't fooling anyone. My vocal problems were not only being heard, they were being discussed among people whose opinions mattered. I realized I had to do something drastic.

After Kim left my office, I called my speech therapist, Dr. Miller, and explained what had just transpired. I asked her whether there was anything she could prescribe to help me calm down, because my anxiety was almost out of control. I asked about Xanax, which I'd heard had helped a great many people experiencing anxiety. She told me she could not prescribe such a drug but would see if she could get in touch with a physician attached to the speech clinic at Georgetown, Dr. Thomas Troost. Within minutes, she called back to say she'd reached Dr. Troost in his car, and that he had returned to the hospital in order to carry on a conference call with me and Dr. Miller. After a forty-five-minute discussion, Dr. Troost said he would be willing to prescribe a very small dose of Xanax, but that he believed the major problem was a lack of breath support. He recommended that I resume weekly speech therapy with Dr. Miller in order to retrain and strengthen my diaphragmatic breathing. I left the station that evening feeling slightly more hopeful. Perhaps Xanax would finally do the trick. But as I was soon to learn, there are no "tricks" that address long-term problems. I used the Xanax for about one week, with no noticeable improvement. I did, however, follow Dr. Troost's advice and returned to Dr. Miller for more breathing and vocal training.

A week or so later, I went back to see my internist of twenty years, Carole Horn, who'd tried many different approaches to my problem. In the third week of February 1998, I asked her about Prozac, and whether she thought it might help me. She was doubtful, but agreed I might try a tiny liquid dose, much smaller than the smallest dose available in pill form. Knowing how sensitive I am to drugs, she urged me to try the Prozac over the weekend, monitor myself extremely carefully, and then, on

Monday, if I was experiencing no side effects, to take a small dose, followed by a cup of caffeinated coffee. She thought the coffee might help me breathe more easily on the air. I should add here that I hadn't had caffeinated coffee in years because of my sleeping problems.

On Monday morning, February 23, 1998, I took a tiny dose (one quarter of a teaspoon) of the liquid Prozac, plus one cup of caffeinated coffee, when I got to the office. Unfortunately, my reaction was extreme. My voice began to shake uncontrollably. I thought I was going to pass out on the air. My strong desire was to get up and run out of the studio. I knew I sounded awful, but there was nothing I could do but get through the two hours. Immediately following the broadcast, there was a car waiting outside to take me to the Four Seasons Hotel, where I was to moderate a panel discussion entitled "Gossip: What's America Talking About?" for Gail Berendzen's outstanding organization called Women of Washington (WW). She had been moved to establish the group after her husband's resignation as president of American University, in an effort to create an atmosphere in which women of all ages, backgrounds, and professional status could come together and support one another. From its very small beginning, WW has now expanded to a West Coast chapter in Los Angeles, and provides guidance and leadership to women of all ages.

The ballroom on that particular day was filled with three hundred people, all waiting to hear the comments of the four panelists, each a prominent journalist whose beat was gossip. The Monica Lewinsky story was front and center, so what at one time in our history would have been relegated to the tabloids was now on the front pages of major newspapers and on television networks throughout the country. My memory is one of profound embarrassment at how terrible my voice sounded that day. I'm certain (though no one has ever told me this) that people were wondering how in the world this moderator could ever have become the host of a national radio program. I can't explain how I managed to get through it, except to say that the panelists were all very talkative and informative. I, on the other hand, found myself dreading the prospect of opening my mouth even to put forward a question. As soon as the event was over, I rushed out of the hotel to the waiting car and drove back to the station, having made up my mind. I walked into my office and asked Sandra Pinkard, my senior producer, to come in and shut the door. In a frantic, trembling voice, I told her I had to take some time off from the show, for just how long I wasn't sure. She was totally taken aback and upset, attempting to convince me that my voice was not as bad as I thought it was. But I knew I had to get out. I felt especially guilty leaving that day, because I had just hired two bright, energetic young women as producers on the show. They'd been on the job for only two weeks. I then went upstairs to tell Kim Hodgson of my decision. With our semi-annual fund drive coming up, which I'd never once missed in over twenty years, I knew he'd be dismayed, but there was nothing I could do. He asked, "How long do you think you'll be gone?" I responded that I had no idea, but that I had to go. Finally, seeing just how distraught I was, he said, "Take as much time as you need."

CHAPTER 26

*F*ORTUNATELY, that very evening I had an appointment with a highly respected psychopharmacologist,
Dr. Susan Fiester, who had agreed to see me on very
short notice. I went to her office at six-thirty, still shaking from
the day's experience. She listened intently as I told her what had
happened. When I finished, she smiled and said, "Congratu-
lations. You've had a full-blown panic attack." We talked for
nearly an hour and a half, and I assured her that all the doctors
I'd seen had insisted there was absolutely nothing of a physical
nature at work. She decided to prescribe Paxil, explaining to me
that my ongoing concern about my voice problems had led to
higher and higher levels of anxiety, combined with depression.
That combination could finally have reached such a peak of
intensity that my speech pattern was being affected. I confessed
to her that my worry over how my voice sounded had even be-

gun to interfere with my thought process, causing me to pause and even hesitate, looking for just the right word and then being afraid that I couldn't utter it.

During that hour and a half, we talked about my background and I told her that until now, I'd always believed that no matter what had to be done, I could do it. I could push my doubts and fears out of my mind and simply do it. I would not allow myself to acknowledge that I felt afraid, or that I wasn't up to the task. But I had come to realize the increasing toll this was taking on my body, particularly as I suffered sleep deprivation and faced the same problems day after day after day. In truth, that evening in Dr. Fiester's office I felt close to what I imagine might once have been called a nervous breakdown.

In addition to prescribing Paxil, Dr. Fiester said that part of the recovery regime for both the anxiety and depression should include cognitive behavioral therapy, a form of treatment I was neither familiar with nor understood, but I was willing to follow her recommendation. She put me in touch with Dr. Laura Primakoff, a psychologist in private practice, whose treatment approach was precisely in the area of cognitive behavioral therapy. I called Dr. Primakoff the next day and she agreed to see me immediately.

Thus began a three-month period, from late February to early May 1998, of daily visits to various therapists. On Mondays and Wednesdays, I had two-hour sessions with Dr. Primakoff, who helped me to begin to understand the ways in which my childhood experiences, plus the pressures of the more immediate past, had integrated themselves into my thought processes as well as my manner of coping. My task with her was to work toward halting the automatic negative thinking with which I was attacking myself, and to undo some of the patterns of behavior that had led to the February 23 "crash." It made complete sense to me as she explained that a lifetime of self-disparagement was constantly at work in me, being countered every step of the way by my stubborn refusal to accept anything less than whatever accomplishment I'd set out to achieve. So, to put this more graphically, one part of me was constantly saying, "You can't do this! You're stupid! You have no talent! You don't belong here! You're a fraud." The other part of me kept repeating, "You can achieve. You are intelligent. You can do this." The awful irony was that the more I succeeded, the louder the negative voices had become. Dr. Primakoff helped me to begin the process of both acknowledging the negative voices and at the same time refusing to allow them to continue to control me with the fear of failure.

We role-played; at times she assumed the negative voice, at other times the caring voice. These were extraordinarily intense sessions, perhaps the most intense I've ever experienced. At one point, as we began to talk about my parents' deaths, and especially my mother's, I began to weep uncontrollably, and continued to sob throughout the entire two hours. After I got home, the crying went on for yet another two hours. Something had opened up from deep within me that could not be shut down again. One reason I believe those two-hour sessions were so intense is that Dr. Primakoff is an extremely vocal and animated person. I'd had lots of therapy in the past but had never encountered a therapist with whom I felt more emotionally in sync.

On Monday afternoons, for about an hour and a half, I saw Ellen Barlow, a young woman whose early ambition to become a ballerina had been dashed when, in a mountain-climbing accident, she broke several bones in her right foot. She then began to study yoga, and progressed from that to other forms of healing, concentrating on breathing, gentle movement, manipulation, and massage of all parts of the body. Ellen's demeanor matches her touch. She has a soft, caressing voice, as well as a caring and gentle manner. She seems to float when she walks, with a movement that seems effortless. My friend Kate Lehrer introduced me to Ellen, and a more appropriate gift for my tension-ridden body I cannot imagine.

As Ellen and I worked together, she pointed out the positioning of my head and the straining in my throat and neck muscles as I talked. She helped correct my posture and, to my surprise, suggested that my exercise device, the Nordic Track, might actually be contributing to the stiffness and tension in my neck, which had reached a point where I could barely turn my head to the left or right. Walking, as we've all been told, and as she underscored, was the best exercise possible, in addition to a special regime of stretching and breathing each morning. All of her suggestions and manipulations helped me to respond more tenderly to my own physical being, something I'd not paid much attention to up until then.

On Fridays, usually for an hour and a half, I saw Dr. Fiester, the psychopharmacologist. Unlike a few other psychiatrists I have known, Dr. Fiester is totally accessible and completely responsive, and prescribes medications extraordinarily carefully. After my first few weeks on Paxil, which is primarily an antidepressive medication but which also assists in dealing with anxiety, she told me that she felt depression was the lesser part of my problem. Paxil also seemed to exacerbate my already disturbed sleep patterns. She now suggested, in addition to Paxil, the introduction of Klonopin (generic clonazepam), an antianxiety medication that would definitely allow me to sleep. I was somewhat reluctant to try mixing two drugs, especially since I was already taking Prilosec (for reflux) and Premarin (to relieve menopausal symptoms). Up until then, I had been reluctant to take even Tylenol, having read some of the literature about its possible side effects on the liver. But Dr. Fiester's reputation as a psychopharmacologist, as well as her thoughtful manner and approach, allowed me to put my trust in her and to follow her recommendations. Indeed, the addition of Klonopin was a great relief, because not only did it reduce the anxiety, but for the first time in years I found myself sleeping through the night.

On Tuesdays and Thursdays, usually for an hour and a half, I saw Dr. Susan Miller, my speech therapist. She helped me to understand the absolute necessity for concentrated breathing, not from the upper chest, as I had been doing, but from the stomach, with the expansion of the rib cage. I remained skeptical of the notion that my voice problems were strictly breath-related, but to my surprise, there were some days when if I really concentrated on the breathing there was virtually no tremor and I could speak relatively smoothly. Dr. Miller explained that the more anxiety I experienced, the more shallow my breathing became, leading to a totally unreliable and unsteady tone coming from my vocal folds.

It was an intensive five-day regime, both exhilarating and exhausting. In addition, I prayed to God constantly to help me to accept His will, whatever it might be. Of course I wanted to be healthy again and to resume my career, but my early religious teaching had instilled in me the idea that one does not ask God directly for healing, but rather receives whatever is His will. I received e-mail and letters telling me that people all over the country were praying for me, and I was greatly encouraged by that knowledge because I have always believed in the power of prayer. St. Columba's Episcopal Church, where John and I had begun to attend services regularly, had also placed me on its prayer list, thanks to the rector, Dr. Jim Donald. The thing about prayer, though, is that your own ideas and wishes may be totally different from what God has in mind for you. I kept reminding myself that it was His will, not mine, that would be done.

During that period between late February and the beginning of May, I saw very few people. My closest friends came by, but I shied away from attending any outside functions. I was embarrassed and nervous and didn't want to be confronted with questions about my health or my voice. I learned later that many people believed I was suffering from throat cancer or had had a stroke and were convinced that I was permanently off the air. I did most of my communicating by e-mail, talking over program subjects with producers, responding to questions from listeners, and writing notes of thanks to well-wishers. I took many long walks, watching as trees began to take on the delicate green of early spring, pausing each day to study the changes occurring in my garden. My work space is located in my sewing room, overlooking the garden, so I would watch the opening of tulips and jonquils from afar and then, at the end of my walk, as I came in through the garden gate, examine them up close.

It was during those long walks that I experienced my strongest feelings of closeness to God. During my adult life, I'd gotten into the habit of offering prayers of thanks many times during the course of each day for small things, such as a glimpse of a beautiful flower, a delicious breeze, or, on a larger scale, the health of my family. I thanked Him for my friends, for the good fortune He'd granted John and me, for our ability to see, and hear, and feel. In addition, I asked Him to guide me, to help me understand what was happening to me, and to help me to accept the outcome, whatever it might be. It was the first time in more than twenty years that I'd had such a long period of time by myself, and while I was worried and anxious, somehow I knew that I would come to regard this period as a very precious time in my life.

One day, my dear friend Jane Dixon, Washington's suffragan bishop, called to tell me that Bishop Ronald Haines, whom I had met on several occasions, had asked her whether I might wish to experience a "laying on of hands," a healing rite of the Episcopal church. I responded that I would be so grateful for that service and would come to the cathedral immediately. When I got there, no more than fifteen minutes later, the two were waiting for me and took me into a tiny, beautiful chapel at Church House, on the cathedral grounds. It was built by a mother in memory of her daughter, and is used by the bishops on special occasions. The three of us sat in the pews talking for a few moments, and then Bishop Haines said, "Well, let us begin." He read a few special prayers from the Book of Common Prayer and then made the sign of the cross on my forehead with holy oil. The two of them laid hands on my head, continuing the prayers, directed very personally toward my voice problems. It was an incredibly moving moment for me, one I shall be ever grateful for.

After that experience, I began to attend St. Columba's Church on a regular basis, going behind the altar with John during the Holy Communion to receive the laying on of hands, administered by those in the parish, ordained or otherwise, each of whom has a special healing ministry. John had done this on several prior occasions, and when I asked why, he said it gave him a sense of spiritual healing. Up to that time, I'd been embarrassed to partake in the healing service, afraid of openly admitting my illness and sense of loss. But after those moments at the cathedral with Jane and Bishop Haines, I finally allowed myself to feel the power of the whole service each Sunday morning, the warmth and support of the congregation, and the beauty of the music through those difficult weeks off the air.

CHAPTER 27

*I*N LATE APRIL, with a feeling of desperation, I once again turned to my internist, Carole Horn. When she heard my voice on the telephone, still in its quivering, unsteady state, she made a decision that surprised and unsettled me. She said emphatically that she wanted me to go to Johns Hopkins University Hospital to see an outstanding neurologist, Dr. Stephen Reich. Dr. Reich, according to Dr. Horn, through a series of tests would be able once and for all to rule out or recognize early signs of Parkinson's disease or amyotrophic lateral sclerosis (ALS), otherwise known as Lou Gehrig's disease. She wrote to him asking him to see me as soon as possible. Though his nurse told me he was completely booked and had just one opening, on July 17, she said she would do what she could to work me in.

Several days later, I received a call from Dr. Reich's scheduler saying that the doctor would see me on Tuesday, May 5, at

8:30 a.m. Then, she said, Dr. Reich wanted me to be examined by Dr. Paul Flint, a head and neck surgeon in the Department of Otolaryngology at Hopkins. So, with considerable fear, John and I made reservations at a hotel in Baltimore for the evening of May 4 so that we wouldn't have to drive over to Hopkins early that morning. We also decided to allow for an extra day in Baltimore in case I was asked to return to Hopkins for further tests.

Here I must make a confession. I was upset with Dr. Horn for insisting on these additional tests, since I'd already undergone an entire battery. After all, I had seen four otolaryngologists, and three neurologists, I'd had an MRI, an MRA, and other neurological examinations. As far as I was concerned, I'd had too many tubes inserted through my nose and throat (a highly unpleasant experience, to say the least), and I had been under the impression that all possibility of a serious neurological disorder had already been ruled out. So her recommendation took me aback. The worst doubts began to overwhelm me. Perhaps this was why none of the medications, nor any of the therapy, had helped my "normal" voice to return. Maybe there was some life-threatening or crippling disease lurking in my body.

We arrived the afternoon prior to my tests and took a long walk around the inner harbor area, enjoying the beautiful weather, the tourists, the boats, and the holiday atmosphere. Then we treated ourselves to a wonderful dinner, and surprisingly (with the help of Klonopin, of course), I slept through the night. When we got to Johns Hopkins at eight-thirty in the morning, I felt like someone about to hear a death sentence. Dr. Primakoff and I had spent a great deal of time helping to prepare me for this visit, and she urged me not to resort to my deeply instilled habit of "catastrophic thinking"—that is, taking a small amount of data and projecting the worst possible outcome. Curiously, where friends and associates are concerned, I'm an optimistic person. But when it comes to worrying about any member of my family or myself, I become more than a little irrational.

Promptly at 9:00 a.m., Dr. Reich came out to greet us in the waiting room. An easy and friendly man, he asked whether I'd mind if several residents, interns, and students were present for the interview and examination. Considering the fact that our daughter, Jennie, and her husband, Russell Zide, had just completed their residency in internal medicine at the Lahey Clinic in Boston, I was sympathetic to the idea of having additional staff along. Dr. Reich had clearly studied all of my previous records that Dr. Horn and I had forwarded to him, but he also wanted to take his own history, and to hear it directly from me. I had brought along the MRI and the MRA taken at Jefferson Hospital in Philadelphia, so he had a full and complete set of background materials.

We were with him for more than an hour, during which he performed several exams, including having me write a sentence on a piece of blank paper, testing my ability to walk a straight line, walk on tiptoe, and walk on my heels, looking at my tongue and palate, and checking my tongue flexibility, my eye and finger coordination, and my reflexes. He then studied the MRI and MRA films and said he wanted to take them down to radiology to check out one detail. His whole entourage followed him, while we returned to the waiting room. In less than ten minutes, he was back. The odd spot on the MRI had turned out to be nothing. He then gave me his diagnosis: essential tremor, confined to the vocal cords. No sign whatsoever of any life-threatening neurological disease, including Parkinson's or ALS. He said the use of moderate amounts of alcohol would reduce the tremor, something I had already discovered on my own. My usual habit for years had been to have two glasses of champagne before dinner. It had become evident to me early on that champagne reduced the tremor and allowed me to speak more freely. He advised me to continue with that regime, as well as with the Paxil. He also said he was going to speak with Dr. Fiester about substituting an anticonvulsant drug called Mysoline (primidone) for the Klonopin. Mysoline is used to treat those who suffer epilepsy, and also tremor. With great relief, we shook hands with all the physicians and left for our second appointment, with Dr. Paul Flint.

When Dr. Flint walked into his examining room where John and I were waiting, he had just come out of surgery of some duration. My first impression was that he had chosen the wrong profession—he looked like a movie star. But within seconds it was clear that he was a very thorough, talented, and compassionate otolaryngologist who was totally absorbed in his work. He had previously spoken with Dr. Miller at Georgetown, who had forwarded all my records to him. I had brought along with me a video of a stroboscopy done at George Washington University in December 1997, hoping that that video would preclude Dr. Flint's having to do another examination of my throat and vocal cords.

After we had talked for about forty-five minutes about the experience with Advil, the appearance of the tremor, and the deterioration of my voice over the past several years, the three of us watched the video together. At the end of the video, Dr. Flint asked me to read two sentences. The first had several *r*'s, *t*'s, and *l*'s in it, and was difficult. Dr. Miller and I knew this was the case because in some of our speech therapy sessions, the same difficulty had become apparent. Then Dr. Flint asked me to read the second sentence, which was much easier and flowed from my tongue and mouth with no difficulty. After I had finished, he gave his considered opinion that I was suffering from spasmodic dysphonia (SD), a condition that affects the muscles that control speech. I was somewhat surprised, but not totally. In fact, during my various examinations with other otolaryngologists, I had even asked whether SD might be the problem. The answer had always been no.

Spasmodic dysphonia of the *ad*ductor type (some refer to it as spastic dysphonia) occurs when the basal ganglia within the brain send an incorrect message to the vocal cord muscles, instructing them to contract too tightly, in some cases blocking speech altogether. In adductor SD, speech may sound strained, quivery, hoarse, jerky, creaky, staccato, or garbled, and can sometimes be very difficult to understand. While my own pattern of speech didn't seem to fit the entire description, there was no question that my voice was strained, quivery, hoarse, and creaky. I asked Dr. Flint whether broadcasters were particularly susceptible. "Not at all," he said. "In fact, I'm treating a doctor, an attorney, and a computer analyst, all of whom suffer the same problem." When I asked him how common a disorder it was, he acknowledged that there is no accurate data since most people who suffer the problem are too ashamed to seek help. Just as I did, they search and search for some external cause, perhaps an allergy or a particular food or beverage, rather than turning to the medical profession.

The less frequently occurring SD is of the *ab*ductor type, in which there is an overcontraction of the muscles that *separate* the vocal cords, resulting in a choppy and breathy whispering voice pattern. This type of SD is apparently far more difficult to treat. For psychological reasons, Dr. Flint said, many of those who experience spasmodic dysphonia of either type try to avoid situations in which they have to talk. In my own case, of course, that would have been impossible if I hoped to keep my job. In fact, for most sufferers of spasmodic dysphonia, the disorder becomes profoundly isolating and depressing. I had experienced anxiety when simply walking into a drugstore and saying my name to order a prescription. Speaking on a telephone had become a huge obstacle, and this is typical of SD sufferers. Unless there was lots of background noise, I could barely order food in a restaurant, and I was embarrassed to try to talk across the table to dinner companions. What many who experience SD finally choose is isolation, rather than subjecting themselves to listening to their struggles to speak.

As for treatments, Dr. Flint and Dr. Reich both strongly recommended periodic injections of botulinum toxin (a bacterial
toxin that paralyzes muscles) into the overactive muscles of the
vocal cords. This is a remedy that for a little more than a decade
has been used successfully in 90 to 95 percent of cases and about
which I had done a fair amount of reading. The alternative to
Botox, as it's called, would be Mysoline, the anticonvulsant
that neurologist Reich had earlier recommended. But Dr. Flint
informed me that Dr. Reich agreed with his diagnosis of spasmodic dysphonia and believed that either drug could be of assistance. Now a choice had to be made. Mysoline could take as long
as four to six weeks just to achieve an effective level in the blood-
stream to counter the dysphonia; only then would we know
whether it would work. Having been off the air for nearly three
months, the idea of having to wait yet another four to six weeks
just to learn whether the drug might help was not appealing.

On the other hand, Botox had to be injected directly into the
neck to reach the vocal cords. Of course, some measure of local
anesthesia would be applied, but the idea of an injection in the
neck did not make me happy. Also, the effects of the Botox injections would wear off in three to six months, meaning that I'd
have to return for more of them periodically, as their beneficial
effects diminished. Dr. Flint explained that if I opted for the
Botox, he would give me a very low dose to begin with. If it
didn't work, it would mean that I'd have to return to Johns Hopkins in a week or two for another injection. In addition, the immediate effects of the Botox would be, ironically, a temporary
but total loss of voice, since the muscles around the vocal cords
would be completely paralyzed, leaving them wide open. When
we speak, our vocal cords come together and vibrate, creating
sound. With Botox, the paralyzed vocal cords are temporarily
left wide open, allowing only the passage of air and the production of a faint whisper. That total whispering phase might last
anywhere from one to four weeks. Also, Dr. Flint said, I might

experience flulike symptoms like nausea and fatigue, which would be indications that the toxin was working.

John and I discussed the options briefly, and I began to ask questions. Was there any possibility, for instance, that the vocal cords might be hurt by these injections, thereby rendering the voice even worse than it was now? Answer: no. Was there any history of damage to the vocal cords after repeated injections of Botox? Answer: no. Was there any danger that after a long period of using Botox and then stopping the injections, the voice could be worse than before the injections began? Answer: no. At that point, I apologized to Dr. Flint for taking up so much of his time with my questions and my indecision. His response profoundly affected me. He said, "I'm here all day for you if you need me to be." With that, I looked at John, who had originally thought Mysoline would be the more conservative and more appropriate approach. Yet when he heard all my questions and realized how much I'd read about Botox, he was prepared to accept my decision. And so, when there were no more questions, Dr. Flint said, "Are you ready, then?" "Yes," I said. "Let's do it."

The first thing Dr. Flint did was discuss the dosage with me. I reminded him of my experience with Advil, and how sensitive my body seemed to be to drugs. He explained that Botox dosage was measured in "mouse units," minute amounts ranging from 0.3 to 0.4 all the way up to two or even three full units per side. We agreed to try a conservative approach, with the understanding that if the desired result was not achieved, I might have to come back for an additional dose. Conversely, if he gave me too high a dose, I might only be able to speak in a whisper for several weeks. He decided to administer the small dose of 0.5 unit per side.

Dr. Flint then applied a series of small disks to my neck and throat area which allowed him to locate on a video screen precisely where the injections should be made so as to reach the muscles involved. He injected a painkiller into the neck area, which left my swallowing mechanism feeling uncomfortably thick and ineffective. Then, after a few moments, he injected the botulinum toxin. As he did so, I found myself praying silently to God for a good outcome. There was some discomfort with the injection, but it was not unbearable. The entire procedure took less than five minutes. John and I then left the hospital, our hands clasped, both of us hoping and trusting that we had finally found the answer. We took a taxi back to our hotel, feeling both grateful for the diagnosis and treatment and relieved that the dreaded possibilities of our trip to Baltimore were behind us. The sun was shining brightly, so we decided to go for a long walk to try to shake off the fear and anxiety that had been with both of us for so many months. Of course, we had no way of knowing whether this would truly work, but at that moment we were placing all our hopes on the knowledge and expertise of doctors whom we felt we could trust. As we left our hotel, we decided to walk and walk and walk. We needed to breathe, to take in the smells of the boats and restaurants and people and water. And somehow, though we'd walked the same walk just the day before, it all seemed brand-new.

When we arrived home the next day, we decided to have a small celebration. There was no guarantee that my voice would recover, but the very fact that more serious diseases or disorders had been ruled out was sufficient cause to raise a toast. We phoned our friends the Busbys and the Lehrers and agreed to meet at one of our favorite restaurants, DeCarlo's. It was a joyous evening, and while I was waiting somewhat impatiently for my voice to disappear (since Dr. Flint said that would be a sign that the Botox was "doing its job"), I realized during the course of that evening that my voice seemed stronger than it had been. When I awoke the next morning, I was disappointed. There was no discernible change in my voice from the previous night, and I began to worry that the Botox, for some reason, wasn't working. It didn't take much to get me into my "catastrophic" mode of imagining either that I'd have to receive another injection or that Botox wasn't going to work for me at all. I went through the day doing ordinary things, praying each time I opened my mouth that there would be no voice at all. Strange, after all those months and years of waiting for a normal voice, to now pray for no voice at all! Finally, at 3:30 a.m. the next morning, I woke up and realized there was absolutely no sound coming from my throat. I was ecstatic and immediately woke John, who shouted "Hallelujah!" We hugged and kissed and he gave me the high five!

CHAPTER 28

*T*HE NEXT FEW DAYS exist in something of a haze in my memory. The flulike symptoms came on with a vengeance. I canceled all therapy appointments since I couldn't talk, and spent the next three days between bed and bathroom, not answering the telephone, sipping tea and broth, and for the most part feeling miserable. But I knew it was all in a good cause. Dr. Flint had indicated to me that the extent of the loss of voice would be an indication of the effectiveness of the Botox, so I managed to convince myself that the flulike symptoms, as bad as they were, were another indication that the Botox was doing its job. I've since learned that the severity of my symptoms was unusual and that most patients have a much milder reaction to Botox. Another drawback was my difficulty in drinking liquids. Because the vocal cords were totally paralyzed, the swallowing mechanism was affected, and from time to time I'd suffer a slight choking sensation. Dr. Flint advised that I take only very small sips of any liquid.

On Friday, May 8, Jodie Allen, a friend and colleague from *Slate* magazine, a daily on-line news magazine, called to see how I was. For years, Jodie has been one of the "regulars" on our "Friday Morning News Roundup," and is one of the smartest women I know. In my barely audible whisper, I let her know about my having finally received a diagnosis; she wished me well and we hung up. Five minutes later, she called again. "We have an assignment for you," she said. "We'd like you to write a one-week diary for *Slate*. Tell us about your experiences with this disorder, and how you're managing your time at home." At first, I was reluctant, not sure I had the energy needed to produce a week's worth of anything that would be useful or interesting. But she persuaded me to take on the challenge, saying *Slate* needed no more than seven or eight paragraphs each day. Finally, I said I would do it if she would do any editing necessary, and she readily agreed.

Then, almost miraculously, on Sunday, May 10, Mother's Day, five days after the injection, the flu symptoms abated and I felt my energy return. Some people regard Mother's Day as a worthless fiction designed to sell cards, flowers, and slinky nightgowns, but I've always had special feelings about the day, probably because I think motherhood is the toughest job in the world. It's the one for which we have the least amount of training, and one that society as a whole claims to strongly support, but until the last several years, the activities and responsibilities of motherhood have been little appreciated or even understood. Now, as more and more women move into the workplace and find themselves juggling careers and parenting, there is a growing realization of the valuable contribution mothers make to the society as a whole. I love every minute of the day: receiving cards and flowers, talking with adult children on the phone, and celebrating with friends. That's the way it's been every year since I first earned the title.

Mother's Day, 1998, will probably stay in my mind as the most memorable I've ever experienced. It was the first one when I couldn't talk. John and I went to church that morning and I couldn't say prayers along with the rest of the congregation. When the music began, I couldn't sing. When it came time to shake hands with and greet our neighbors in the pew, I could only mouth the words. When the rector asked how I was, I had to struggle to whisper in his ear. It seemed like a bad joke for someone who'd spent the last twenty years as a radio talk-show host, but as soon as my spirits began to sink, I would remind myself that I was actually in a healing process.

I once sprained my ankle out in California at a Public Radio Conference. When I returned home from Washington, I had to emerge from the plane in a wheelchair. The view, as I quickly realized, was very different from that confining device, and people looked at me with curiosity. I wanted to explain to all of them that this wasn't the way I normally got around. I found myself, for the very first time, understanding what it feels like to be different. In the same way, the total absence of my voice during that two-week period shifted my way of thinking, in that I began to develop a greater appreciation not only for the noises of the world around me but also for silence. I found myself listening more closely, especially as I returned to my routine of daily walks. I've always loved to hear the singing of birds, but now there were patterns of bird sounds I began to notice. I spotted a bright red male cardinal on one of these walks, singing his heart out to a duller-colored, but no less beautiful, female, sensing that I might not have listened so intently or heard so clearly had I not experienced my own silence. The realization that I was actually enjoying the experience of silence came as something of a surprise to me, having virtually spent a lifetime going out of my way to avoid it.

I tried to put as much as possible of those feelings into the *Slate* diary. What I realized was how wonderful it was to be writing again, to put ideas down on paper and to have people react to them. Each day, I sent off the diary to Jodie, and each day she promptly responded with encouragement. Once the first installment went up on *Slate*'s Web site, I began hearing from people who also suffered from spasmodic dysphonia. In fact, the National Spasmodic Dysphonia Association got in touch with me, offering me information, all kinds of assistance, and, most important of all, encouragement. It really lifted my spirits to be in touch with people who knew exactly what I was experiencing. I also heard from listeners to the program, who'd wondered about my absence and were effusive in their kind words and praise for my "going public" with my illness. I must admit it had never occurred to me not to reveal the problem, once I found out what it was. I felt as though I owed it to my listeners, who'd been so loyal to me over the years, to be honest about what had happened. What I received in turn cannot be measured.

The silence lasted two full weeks. During that period, I could barely whisper. When I had something to say to John, he would put his ear next to my mouth so he could hear it. In fact, he claimed he became very fond of that approach to communication, saying he felt it created a kind of special intimacy between us. But answering the telephone was a real problem, a strain not only for me but for those on the other end of the line. Though most of my closest friends knew what was happening, others who had not read the *Slate* diary were concerned about my absence from the air and baffled by my lack of voice. Rumors were continuing to circulate that I was suffering from some fatal disease, but all I could do was to answer questions as they came to me. As with any other ailment, most people were reluctant to ask direct questions, so their imaginations ran wild. Meanwhile, the station kept saying, again and again, "She's having voice problems."

By the start of the third week, soft sounds began to emerge from my vocal cords. What little there was of my voice sounded very strained, with mostly air coming through, creating an intensely breathy quality. But, nevertheless, some measure of sound was an improvement. I spoke with Dr. Flint frequently, giving him updates on my condition and remarking on how hard it was to get out even a very few words because of the number of breaths required. He urged me to have patience.

I spent a great deal of time at the computer during those weeks, communicating with people all over the world. But it was a different kind of communication because I couldn't see into my correspondent's eyes. I would try to imagine the face of the person I was in touch with, wondering about the cast of the eyes, the tilt of the eyebrows or shoulders or neck in response to a particular comment. I'd always said that going into the studio to interview a guest each morning was like learning to dance with a new partner, sensing when to lead and when to follow. E-mail, for all its advantages, allowed me to remain in touch but lacked some of the sheer pleasure I've always experienced through direct human contact. I managed to make the best of it, however.

One day, a friend at National Public Radio, Martha Raddatz (who's now with ABC-TV), called and suggested we have lunch together sometime soon. We set a date, but when the time came, I realized I still had no voice other than a faint whisper, so I suggested an alternative: that we have a virtual lunch, with each of us seated before her computer, permitting the words and messages to fly back and forth, even though some might overlap. I never imagined how much fun it would be. I loved her use of language, I laughed at some of her observations, and I felt her concern for me. Yes, I missed looking into her face, reacting to her choice of food, sharing the animation, but nevertheless it worked. When I mentioned the idea to someone else, he said he was going to set up a virtual breakfast with a friend of his. It was friendship, both virtual and real, that I felt in those weeks and months away from my job, and it was both glorious and over-whelming. Of course, I knew I could count on my family and my very closest friends, but I had no idea there would be such an out-pouring of concern from people I'd never met. So many com-mentators have lamented the demise of good relationships, but in my view, friendship is alive and well.

As the sounds emanating from my vocal cords increased, my depression and anxiety began to subside. Of course, I remained on a small dose of an antidepressant as well as an antianxiety medication, but I began to regain a feeling of optimism that somehow, someday, this crisis would be resolved. It took two more full weeks before I had something that could really be called a voice. I continued in close communication with Dr. Flint during that period, and he noted a strengthening and greater resonance each time we spoke. He assured me that the improve-ment would continue in the next few weeks, with noticeable incremental tone each day. And, thank heavens, he was right.

On June 11, 1998, after nearly four months off the air, I went back to the program. (During that period, a series of people hosted the program for me, including columnist Steve Roberts, Susan Page of *USA Today*, Jim Angle of Fox News, and Tom Gjelten of NPR. Daily decisions as to topics and guests were made by the producers and me through frequent e-mail.) The voice was shaky, but strong enough to carry on, and the warm reception from listeners made me happy and relieved. During the previous week, I had come to the studio several times during off-hours just to get a feel for the place again and to sit at the microphone. You'd think that after having done this work for so long, I could jump right back in, but my therapists convinced me of the need to reenter the work sphere gradually, and to allow myself to experi-ence the anxiety of moving back into the broadcast chair.

Anxiety is an extraordinary state of mind. I had lived with it for so long and in so many different situations, but I had hardly ever allowed myself to acknowledge it fully, either to myself or to others. I would just keep saying to myself, "I can do this, whatever it is." What I learned during that period off the air, seeing therapists almost every day, was that if I were to keep operating in that same fashion without looking anxiety directly in the eye and dealing with it, it would somehow, someday, get the best of me. So instead of pretending that I could do everything I had to do, no matter how great the fear, I had to learn to listen more attentively to my internal voices, and to acknowledge them.

The week after I returned to the broadcast, I invited all of my therapists on the air to do a program on spasmodic dysphonia. As Dr. Flint and Dr. Miller described the range of symptoms and the difficulties they caused, the phone lines began to light up. Clearly, there were many people listening to the broadcast who'd experienced similar problems and had either been diagnosed with spasmodic dysphonia or had simply been told they were "anxious" or experiencing a case of "nerves." It was clear that there was great interest in the subject since more than one hundred people called to order a cassette copy of the show.

CHAPTER 29

*H*OW CURIOUS, after a career of listening intently and attentively to others, to finally come to a place where I have had to learn to become more alert to my own feelings and sensibilities. Even as I write this, I experience a certain exasperation with myself. After all, one would think that at the age of sixty-two, I would have learned all this by now. But what I realize is that I'm just beginning to understand—in part thanks to the therapy I've had, but also in part because of the act of writing it all down on paper—just how much I really don't know about why I react to certain situations in certain ways, and how those reactions can affect what happens next. What has long been buried can have a profound effect. Old patterns and ways of thinking become almost automatic in the brain. Extreme self-criticism, for example, has become a learned behavior in my case, and while it may have been useful in the creation of a radio program, it has, at times, been very difficult to bear.

———

My judgmental inner voice has also extended to others. During those periods of my life when I felt least secure about myself and judged myself harshly, I turned that attitude toward my family and friends. It's how I was treated, and, eventually, how I began to treat other people. This is not an easy thing to acknowledge to myself or to others, yet I feel a certain relief in recognizing what that attitude has been in the past, and working to bring about a change. I'm not stuck forever in the patterns of childhood. As I've struggled to gain some maturity and felt the kindness of others, it's helped me to recognize how much more comfortable it feels to quiet those judgmental voices, to learn to be less critical of the actions of those around me, and to allow myself a little more slack in the process.

Fear of failure goes right along with that, and for too long I regarded my voice problems as an indication of failure. For example, Dr. Primakoff has worked with me a great deal on my tendency toward "catastrophic thinking," when I turn an ordinary situation into something disastrous. Ordinary worry is one thing; believing that something awful has happened to your husband or your children every time they're half an hour late is another. Until a diagnosis was made, I saw my voice problems as not only bringing my career to an abrupt end but taking away everything I had come to value about myself. I blamed myself, thinking there was something I was doing or had done to deserve this outcome. What both Dr. Primakoff and Dr. Fiester have helped me learn is how to manage those feelings, to look them in the eye instead of stuffing them away deep inside me. By acknowledging the feeling, I can deal with it. When I stuff it down, it festers, and grows into something even more catastrophic.

One of the most urgent questions I asked myself during those months when my voice problems were becoming more apparent to me and others was not "Why me?" Rather, it was "Why now?" After nearly twenty years of daily broadcasting with what I acknowledge was not the usual professional-sounding radio voice, why should this kind of difficulty have hit now? Was it, as many had suggested, simply the result of an overwhelming sched-ule made up of trying to meet too many demands—professional, social, and personal—that left too little room for relaxation, from morning till night? If so, why hadn't many others who work just as hard and just as long as I in this demanding city succumbed as well? Was it, ironically, the result of growing anxiety over the success of the program? An almost irrational need to keep prov-ing myself, even though people all over the country had wel-comed the program into their homes, offices, and cars?

It remains a question I cannot answer, except to say that I find that my habits are changing, in small ways. I no longer drag myself out of bed at 5:00 a.m. I allow myself to sleep until 5:45 or 6:00 a.m. on most weekday mornings. I no longer use a Nordic Track because it irritates my neck muscles; instead, I've begun a program of exercise and weight lifting at a health club directly across the street from our studios at WAMU. My husband and I go out fewer nights of the week and get more rest. We're trying to plan occasional short trips for ourselves, to allow for brief breaks from the stress of the daily regime.

The relationship between John and me has undergone a tremendous change in the last few years. First of all, after nearly forty years of marriage, we've learned to live with each other. That seems like such a simple thing to say, but we are two ex-traordinarily different people, in both temperament and tastes. In the beginning, every issue seemed like a tug-of-war to deter-mine who would "win" and who would "lose." Over the years, the notion of winning or losing has become less important and, I'm glad to say, has finally disappeared. Instead, the forces draw-ing us together—two children we both adore and the pride we've taken in them, the support we've needed and given to each other during times of particular job or health-related stress, and the therapy we've had together and individually—have finally given us the marriage we both wanted when we set out together in 1959. We've learned tolerance for the other's point of view. We've learned to change our language and tone toward each other so as to make our points without tearing the other one down. That's required us to learn to trust each other in ways that, in the early years, we simply couldn't do. And there was sheer stubbornness, mostly on my part. After one failed marriage, I was not prepared to experience another. I also believed that, no matter how painful the marriage, our children would have suffered significantly from divorce. John has also come to realize that living a solitary life would have been disastrous for him, and that our relationship has given him a security he never saw in his own parents' marriage.

Another aspect of the healing process between us has been the continued strong physical attraction we've felt toward each other. It was, at times, the only way we had to reach out, and became a kind of lifeline through which we could connect with each other. Not only were those moments of exquisite passion, they were moments of joy when we could even laugh at our foolishness and at how ridiculous our arguments were. We've learned over the years to pick our battles more selectively, to walk away from some completely and, at times, just to keep quiet. I can remember a number of occasions when, instead of lashing out at a particular word or action, I've just kept my mouth shut. It's amazing how quickly anger can dissipate once I've stepped away from it and plunged into some completely different activity. I thank God that we were able to maintain our marriage. We would have lost so much if we had broken our vows to each other.

CHAPTER 30

IN THE MIDDLE of July of 1998, I began to sense that my voice was giving way again. There was that slight tremor making itself known and beginning to get in the way of my thinking process. I phoned Dr. Flint to see whether he felt it was time for another injection. His own impression as he listened was that my voice was relatively strong, and that it would be better to wait until after John and I returned from an upcoming two-week vacation. Indeed, when we returned from our trip and I went back on the air on August 3, there was no apparent problem. But as the following week wore on, the tremor and the "cracks" in my voice became more noticeable. So I set up an appointment with Dr. Flint for a second injection of Botox on August 19, just three and a half months after the first. This time, Dr. Flint reduced the dosage by one third, taking me down to 0.3 unit in each vocal fold. Despite that reduction, the breathy period again lasted for almost five weeks. On February 26, 1999,

I received the smallest injection yet: o.1 in each vocal fold. After just one week off the air, my voice was strong enough for me to return to the program. Further experimentation with Botox will continue to take place over the next few months, as we search for that "magic" dose that will enable me to return to the air almost immediately after an injection.

A number of people have asked me whether I feel angry that so many medical professionals missed the diagnosis of spasmodic dysphonia, but I've always believed that medicine is a true mixture of art and science. Yes, I did see a number of doctors, and, yes, I did ask several of them whether they thought I might have spasmodic dysphonia. It is conceivable that had I received the diagnosis earlier, I might have been spared some of the anxiety and depression. I've also come to learn that there is a fine line between true spasmodic dysphonia and what some otolaryngologists regard as "muscular dysphonia," a tightening of the tongue and vocal cord muscles that is not quite regarded as spasmodic dysphonia. Perhaps my own case falls somewhere between the two, and because of my experience and the publicity I've received, physicians and speech therapists will now pay closer attention to muscular dysphonia and treat it more quickly with Botox, which in some cases may offer more rapid relief from symptoms than ongoing speech therapy. But I also believe that timing is everything, and that the four-month break I had from the program was beneficial. It allowed me to step back, to learn to listen to my inner voices, to understand the intensity of my own drive, and to delve into some of the forces urging me forward.

Had I not managed to push through those first slight voice tremors in 1992 and stay on the air, "The Diane Rehm Show" might never have had the opportunity to reach a national or international audience. If I had taken a leave of absence back then, NPR might have regarded me as an unreliable choice to host a national broadcast. The tremors themselves didn't prove to be the obstacle, but as the tension over their presence increased,

I was finally forced to make the decision to leave the air. By then, the audience across the country had become accustomed to my voice patterns, and had come to regard them as part of who I was. All of which leads me to believe that there are very few accidents in this world. My faith tells me that I have spasmodic dysphonia for a reason. That reason may be to help educate others about a problem that makes people feel such shame and embarrassment that they choose not to talk at all.

In July 1998, Dr. Susan Miller and I held the first meeting of a support group for individuals suffering from spasmodic dysphonia. We expected ten to fifteen people; about fifty showed up. Some had received Botox and found it a remarkable "cure." Others had been less successful. We shared experiences and information, heard voices better and worse than mine, and listened to some heart-wrenching stories.

Support groups like these exist all over the country, assisted by the National Spasmodic Dysphonia Association (1-800-795-6732). The amount of information provided by that organization, and on the World Wide Web (NSDA@aol.com), regarding both dysphonia and related dystonias is remarkable. As with other illnesses, individuals around the country are finding that the Web can be an enormously helpful source of information, with news of the latest treatments and seminars traveling far and wide in an instant. What we know as of now is that there are no "cures," but there are researchers working around the world to find the answers. I pray for all of us that someday soon, they'll emerge.

Over the past few months, I've wondered a great deal to what extent my childhood and early adult experiences might have contributed to the disorder I'm dealing with now. After all, I was instructed to prepare for a life in the home and I have developed a career. I was told to keep quiet, and here I am, a radio talk-show host. I was told not to tell secrets, and here I am, writing a book. I was subjected to the silence of my mother, and allowed myself to be subjected to the silence of my husband. Did I, in some way, bring all of this on myself as a kind of self-punishment for somehow betraying my parents? Did I unconsciously yearn to be silenced, as a way of reestablishing my place as a "good girl," rather than risk the anger of the inner parent I carry within me? These are questions I'll most likely never find answers to. Instead, I think it's more productive for me to continue to work, through therapy, on both my inner and outer voices, to improve the voice that others hear when I speak and the voice that I hear within my heart.

Not long ago, I decided to buy a gold chain on which to hang a delicate pendant John had bought for me on our first trip to London. I told the jeweler what I was looking for and brought the pendant along with me. He said he'd order it for me and would call me in several days. When he did, I returned to his shop, taking with me not only the London piece but the tiny lavaliere that my mother had given me before she died. I hadn't worn that piece for at least twenty years. I didn't even think about it, I just took it with me. When I got to the jeweler's and he produced the chain, instead of putting it on with the pendant, I slipped the lavaliere on. It was perfect, and I walked out of the shop wearing it.

Several hours later, I went to see Dr. Fiester, and for one brief moment, she had to interrupt our conversation to take a call. It was in that moment that I put my hand to my neck and suddenly realized that after all these years of struggling with the memory of my mother, my anger toward her as well as my feelings of guilt over her death, my wearing of that lavaliere was a symbolic gesture of both acceptance and freedom, a coming to terms with who and what she was, and how my life had been affected by her. I shared my insight immediately with Dr. Fiester, and wondered aloud why it had taken me hours to realize the connection between my wanting to wear the lavaliere and my sense of what it signified. She explained that there are times when we act without knowing why, only that the time is right. This was clearly one of those times.

I know that if I choose to blame myself for my disorder, I can do so and wallow in self-pity. Or, as Dr. Primakoff urges me to do, I can say, firmly, "Stop. That is an unproductive thought." Blaming myself is a hard habit to break, but I'm working on it. I'm also learning to enjoy silence rather than to fear it. Those weeks and months of being without a voice have given me a new appreciation for the silence I used to dread. I can use that silence to reflect on and be in that moment, rather than to run in fear from it. I can now look back and see how important silence has been in my life, and how I have only now begun to transform it from a negative into a positive element. In fact, experiencing silence has become the key to finding my voice.

Recently, our son, daughter-in-law, Nancy, and grandson came to be with us to celebrate Nancy's birthday. Toward the end of the dinner, David asked me how my book was coming along and whether I planned to include a look ahead as well as a look back. As is often the case, he made me think before I could answer. When I did, the response came almost in spite of myself. Having lived most of my life thinking that it was risky to look forward, especially because of my mother's death at forty-nine and my father's at sixty-two (my age at this moment), I've come to count each day as a gift beyond anything I ever expected. I wouldn't go back to change a thing. I am who I am because of what I've experienced. Of course I would prefer not to have encountered spasmodic dysphonia. At the same time, I know that the illness has provided me with an opportunity to examine aspects of my life that I might otherwise have neglected. As for my career, I'm nearing an age when many if not most people are retiring, but I'm not ready to focus on what life would be like without the daily pleasure of bringing some new voice or idea to radio. With people like Barbara Walters, Mike Wallace, Dan Schorr, Andy Rooney, and others going on long past what we used to think of as their "prime" and still regarded as valued contributors to the broadcast world, I'm not prepared to call it quits just because of the calendar. Also, as the population ages, I believe many will welcome hearing more mature voices on the air. As long as my brain and my voice are functioning satisfactorily, I want to continue my efforts to bring listeners civilized discussions about tough issues.

Of course, I have no idea what my voice will sound like tomorrow. Right now, it's strong, and people have commented on its transformation over the past several months. In fact, listeners around the country who had never heard the program until three years ago didn't realize how different my "normal" voice sounded from the one they've been hearing. One person sent me an e-mail from Arizona saying simply, "Wow!" The treatments I've received, in combination with the drugs I'm taking, allow me to be optimistic. Researchers all over the world are looking for a cure for SD, but at this writing, Botox is what's working for me and many others. In addition, I continue to receive speech therapy, attempting to undo many of the bad speaking habits I developed as a result of acquiring SD, such as not breathing frequently enough. I'm also learning to counter negative thoughts more successfully, thanks to Dr. Primakoff and Dr. Fiester.

As for public radio, it will continue to grow—of that I'm sure. The pressures to become more like commercial radio, with more and more "underwriting" announcements, are also likely to increase. The growth of cable and the Internet, plus C-Span Radio, will all compete to attract listeners and viewers. At the same time, people spend hours in their cars, commuting to the workplace, carpooling, or doing errands. So for the foreseeable future, public radio has a solid and growing base. We are an oasis from the sheer noise to be found on much of the radio dial, which makes me believe I have a contribution to make for the time being. I think there will always be a need, indeed a desire, for good, straightforward, honest dialogue, and I'll try to provide that for as long as I am able. Much will depend on the success of the treatments I receive for SD. My voice does matter, but only to a certain extent. If it's not perfect, that's OK. If it becomes distracting, that's not OK. Having always been my own most severe critic, I think I'll know before anyone else tells me when it's time to hand over the microphone. Until that moment, I'll keep working to bring the very best voice I can to public radio.

ℋcknowledgments

FIRST, MUCH APPRECIATION to Carol Beach, a young woman I've known since she was a child, who I have been fortunate enough to have work with me as a producer, and who encouraged and helped me to get this project off the ground. To Ron Goldfarb, my agent, who believed I had a story to tell and then nudged me along, urging me to forgo social occasions and just write, write, write. I want him to know I did manage to get out of the house a few times in the past eighteen months. To Jane Dixon, or, more formally, the Right Reverend Jane Dixon, for our daily 7:00 a.m. phone conversations, during which she laughed and cried with me, always reminding me of her love for me and my family. To the rest of "the Jacks," Carolyn, Gwendolyn, and Carlin. It all started at St. Patrick's. To Mary Beth and David Busby, generous friends, "partners-in-law," as David likes to call us, with whom we've shared so much in the past thirty years, and to their sons, David and Jack, who've taught us all so much about what it means to be loving human beings. To E. J. and

Roger Mudd, supporters, strong allies, and caring friends, who've nourished my soul in so many ways. To Kate Lehrer, who took the time and effort to read my manuscript and offer superb suggestions in the midst of writing her own fourth novel and planning her daughter's wedding; and to Jim Lehrer, whose extraordinary example of the writing life sets a very high standard.

Thanks to Ann Stonehill, who knew exactly what the title for this book should be, and who helped me through the agonies of the writing process. To Michael Nitka, who took a chance in hiring me at WAMU, and then gave me the freedom to shape the program. To Irma Aandahl, who offered her wise counsel and a hand up. She set an example that I shall do my best to continue to follow; and to Susan Harmon, woman of supreme strength, energy, and creativity, plus the will to see her dreams fulfilled.

I am grateful for the memory of Barclay Brown, who died much too soon and left such a void in the lives of all those who loved him. He reminded me to laugh and play, and to enjoy each moment.

My appreciation to Dr. Carole Horn, internist; Dr. Susan Miller, speech pathologist; Dr. Susan Fiester, psychopharmacologist; Dr. Laura Primakoff, behavioral therapist; massage therapist Ellen Barlow; otolaryngologist Dr. Paul Flint; and neurologist Dr. Stephen Reich. They were as strong a team of physicians and healers as I could possibly have asked for, who worked together and separately to help me heal.

My gratitude to the clergy and people of St. Columba's Church in Washington, D.C. They received my husband and me with warm and open hearts, praying with us each Sunday morning for the gift of healing.

Thanks to my sister, Georgette, who shared her memories with me, and in doing so created an opportunity for us to find our way back to sisterhood.

I want to thank the producers of "The Diane Rehm Show," without whose dedication and industry the program would not have achieved its success. I've been blessed with a series of first-rate people who've worked with me, starting with Ann Strainchamps, all of whom in the early days began as volunteers. Brigid McCarthy worked with me for almost five years before moving on to National Public Radio. Richard Paul, now a special projects producer at WAMU, worked with me for a year. Darcy Bacon graduated from volunteer to producer at a crucial moment, along with Maggie Redfern. Darcy stayed nine years. Like Carol Beach, who now works with Hillary Rodham Clinton, and Sandra Pinkard, who remains as a producer after five years, each of these women has been an outspoken promoter of the program. The newest additions to the staff, Elizabeth Terry, Anne Adams, and Nancy Robertson, continue in the same tradition, bringing their energy, enthusiasm, and excellent ideas to the program. Also, thanks to dear friend and supporter Stephen Yasko, who helped launch our national effort. Radio programs don't get on the air without engineers, and there again I've been very fortunate, especially during these past few years. Mike Byrnes, our chief engineer, has also been my computer wizard, always willing to help when I thought the whole book had been sucked out into cyberspace. On a daily basis, Bruce Youngblood, Karen McManus, and Toby Schreiner have all done their best to make me sound good, even under the most difficult of circumstances. My gratitude to WAMU's manager, Kim Hodgson; program director, Steve Martin; and public relations manager, Donna Clark, who, confronted with the vocal difficulties that have afflicted me recently, have stood by with helping hands, encouraging me to take care of my health first and foremost. Also, to Kim's executive assistant, Anne Healy, always solicitous and understanding. My thanks to Sharon Repta for her photographs of Salman Rushdie, Jimmy Carter, Newt Gingrich, and Art Buchwald in the WAMU studio.

To Lee and George Dolgin, there isn't enough space to express the love both John and I feel for you. You brought us together, you helped us through the early years, and you've provided a wonderful example of a mutually supportive relationship.

I've also been fortunate to have met and worked with my editor, Robert Gottlieb. He's been my guide, my cajoler, my challenger, and my analyst. One night early in the writing process, as we talked on the phone just before my bedtime, Bob urged me to consider carefully just how revealing I was prepared to be about my own life and that of my family. I went to sleep after that phone call and dreamed that someone had come into my bedroom and was whitewashing the walls. It was the first of many "wake-up" calls Bob would deliver in his effort to help me learn to articulate not only clearly but honestly. At Knopf, thanks to Ken Schneider, Karen Deaver, Kathleen Fridella, Claire Bradley Ong, Cassandra Pappas, Paul Bogaards, and Jill Morrison.

I want to thank our children, David and Jennie, for the privilege of watching them grow into generous and loving human beings. Parents are sometimes disappointed in their children, but David and Jennie have done nothing other than earn our absolute admiration. I know without a doubt that they and their respective spouses, Nancy Rehm and Russell Zide, as teachers and physicians, will make this a better world. I also want to welcome Alex Rinehart and Remee Klos into our family, with open arms and love.

Finally, many thanks to my partner and husband of nearly forty years, John ("Scoop") Rehm. I look back with amazement, and wonder how it could have gone by so quickly. We have been fortunate, you and I, to have loved and fought and grown and seen it through. We've learned much from each other, and I pray that we continue that process for many years to come.

A Note on the Type

The text of this book was set in Granjon, a type named in
compliment to Robert Granjon, a type cutter and printer active
in Antwerp, Lyons, Rome, and Paris from 1523 to 1590.
Granjon, the boldest and most original designer of his time,
was one of the first to practice the trade of typefounder
apart from that of printer.

Linotype Granjon was designed by George W. Jones, who
based his drawings on a face used by Claude Garamond
(ca. 1480–1561) in his beautiful French books. Granjon more
closely resembles Garamond's own type than do any of the
various modern faces that bear his name.

Composed by Creative Graphics,
Allentown, Pennsylvania
Printed and bound by Quebecor Printing,
Fairfield, Pennsylvania
Designed by Cassandra J. Pappas

QUESTIONS TO PONDER

For reading groups and students, these questions provide some provocative points for group discussion. For individuals, they provide some thoughtful questions to consider as you read *Finding My Voice*.

1. The early years of Diane's book discuss her difficulties in separating her two "worlds": the hostile world of home and the friendly world of school, teachers, and friends. To what extent could you identify with the events of her early life?
2. Diane attributes her mother's remoteness to depression and anger. How did you react to Diane's descriptions of her mother?
3. Did you feel a certain sympathy for her mother, Eugenie, considering the fact that she apparently agreed to marry Wadie even though she was already engaged to someone else?
4. And what about Diane's father? He remains far more in the background than her mother. What role did he play in Diane's upbringing?
5. Diane's relationship with her older sister, Georgette, was not warm. And yet Georgette supported Diane when the issue of membership in a sorority came up. Why do you believe they fought so much and so bitterly? How can sisters have such different memories of their childhood?
6. Diane's first marriage to an Arab American occurred as her mother was dying. Did you feel Diane was pressured into an early marriage?
7. What kind of relationship do you think Diane had with her first husband?
8. When Diane left the Postal Inspection Service for the State Department, her life seemed to undergo change. What are the factors you think contributed to that change?
9. Where did Diane's courage to leave that marriage come from? Or was it selfishness, rather than courage?
10. The Arab-American community was shocked and hurt by Diane's decision to divorce her husband. Should she have stayed in the marriage for the sake of her society?
11. When Diane first met John, she seemed turned off by him. What do you think happened to change her mind?
12. Did you feel there was a flirtation going on between them, even as Diane was trying to ignore this man who was so loud?

13. A loud voice can be a sign of insecurity. Does it seem to you that John Rehm was insecure?
14. Why do you think John proposed to Diane and then said he'd "forgotten"? Do you think he really wanted to marry her?
15. Despite their happy wedding ceremony and reception, two sad things happened: first, Diane fell on the way to the reception; second, the photographer never showed up. All weddings have some imperfections, as do many of the rites of passage in people's lives. Discuss the meaning of rites of passage in your life.
16. After their first child arrived, John and Diane seemed to grow apart. Why do you think that happened to them? Do you think it tends to happen often in marriages?
17. Did Diane come across to you as a sympathetic mother? Or did she do herself and her family a disservice by staying at home for fourteen years?
18. Once she got out of the house and into volunteer work, Diane seemed to come into her own. How did that affect her relationship with her husband and children?
19. The incident of the checkbook seems significant. What did you make of it?
20. Was Diane's start at the radio station pure luck?
21. How far did "luck" take her?
22. Diane experienced extreme self-doubt as she was becoming increasingly well-known. Why do you believe the self-doubt persisted in the face of her success?
23. What about John, and his reactions to her success?
24. Diane began to display her long-standing vocal problems just as her program was going "national." How significant was the timing of that onset to the national distribution of The Diane Rehm Show?
25. What about religion and spiritual faith? How important were they to Diane? And to you?
26. In the end, do you believe that Diane finally forgave her mother? Do you believe she finally came to identify with her mother's own courage?

Visit Capital's website, *www.capital-books.com* for other inspiring books on personal development.